CUSTODIANS OF THE GRASSLANDS

GRASSLANDS

Regeneration, Renewal, Recovery

COLIN SEIS

Shooting Star Press

First published in Australia in 2022

Shooting Star Press

PO Box 6813, Charnwood ACT 2615

info@shootingstar.pub

www.shootingstar.pub

ABN 63 158 506 524

A catalogue record for this book is available from the National Library of Australia.

Seis, Colin.

Custodians of the Grasslands

ISBN 978-1-925821-73-4 Paperback

ISBN 978-1-925821-74-1 E-Book

Edited by Katie Taylor

Cover Design & Typesetting by Cath Brinkley

CONTENTS

HARRY

On the 24th August 1999 my father Harry Seis died aged 86, leaving a great legacy and a life that his ancestors would have been proud of, and his descendants are exceedingly indebted to.

My father had a significant influence on me. He was very innovative, and encouraged me to think for myself, never discouraging me from doing new things, although he did advise against some of my more 'ratbag' ideas. He was very supportive of my suggested change in the way we should graze our sheep and could immediately see the benefits of Pasture Cropping. Without his support, it is doubtful if Pasture Cropping would have ever achieved its full potential.

Harry was born in 1912 on 19th December. From a young age he excelled, and always did things differently. As a teenager he shone at sport, particularly cricket, but his greatest sporting achievement was to be in athletics. During the 1920s races were very popular around the bush and Harry was known to beat all comers. By the time he was ten he was trapping rabbits and selling the skins to buy his own pair of running spikes. At age thirteen he went to High School in Western Sydney because there was very little higher education available in country areas. While at school in Sydney his athletic ability was noticed and he was soon on the NSW schoolboy squad becoming 100 Yard NSW champion and NSW High Jump champion. He was destined for greater things, invited to go to England for professional training with Olympic potential being suggested. However this was not to be. His father Joseph needed him at home to help with farm work. I have often wondered if he ever had regrets at not being given a chance to be an Olympian.

By the time he was 18, he had leased land and grew his first wheat crop using his father's horse team and farming equipment. At 19 he began farming using methods that were unique, being amongst the first to use chemical fertiliser to enhance the growth of his wheat crop. In the 1940s he started what is believed to be the first country school bus and again in the 1940s was one of the very first to use introduced 'improved pasture' and further improved the pastures production with the use of chemical fertiliser (superphosphate) on pastures. It was also in the 1940s that he started using a technique that was to be the forerunner of Pasture Cropping.

Harry was very influential in the stud Merino industry and was involved in the establishment of three merino studs on Winona and my brother Ian's property, Roxanna. He was an exceptional sheep judge, with his expertise on sheep breeding being sought Australia wide.

By using his knowledge of merino sheep breeding and pasture improvement he developed Winona into a very profitable and successful property, using and following the best science and advice that was available to him.

As well as his work in agriculture he gave a lifetime of dedicated work to the community. This community work included involvement with the Gulgong show society for 63 years of which he served nine terms as president. Harry was a member of the Birriwa bushfire brigade for 60 years, many of these as Fire Captain, and was instrumental in the success of the world-renowned Gulgong historical museum, being president for 13 years and committee member for 27 years.

It was the work he did with children that he loved most and was involved with the Gulgong Red Hill Field studies centre teaching school children about agriculture and Australian rural history.

As a result of this enormous contribution to Gulgong and the regional community, he was awarded with the medal of the Order of Australia (OAM) in 1990.

Harry has been sadly missed by all who knew him, but no one missed him more than my mother Mari, who 60 years earlier married Harry, came to Gulgong and never left.

Mari lived to the age of 92 before dying of a broken heart in 2005.

This book is for them.

REGENERATION

T his book is about the family property, 'Winona'; its decline during one hundred and fifty years of agricultural land use, and how the healing process was started. The healing can be likened to restoring a badly damaged Rembrandt. Most can be fixed, some we need to paint ourselves.

The story of an Australian farming family's journey from the late 1700s until today and about how I, developed and adopted agricultural methods that restored 'Winona', back to productive, profitable native grassland.

While the First Nations peoples were custodians of Australia and her grasslands 2000 years ago, around the Mediterranean Sea and the Middle East the so-called civilised people of the world were systematically destroying their grasslands, soil and civilisations while developing what was to become modern agriculture.

Was the way we farmed around the world flawed from the start? Why did Indigenous populations around the planet develop a culture of nurturing the land? Why did most of these Indigenous people have a spiritual connection to the land? Why do we, 2000 years later, not learn from the world's native people? Why do we continue to use agricultural

5

practices that, in the past, destroyed the great civilisations of the world?

We have been led to believe that technology will solve all of our agricultural and ailing planetary problems, but so far all that technology has done is to speed up our destruction. The use of 300 horsepower tractors, one hundred feet wide machinery and an array of poisonous herbicides and pesticides designed to kill anything that gets in the way, is destroying ecosystems everywhere.

Are we to experience the same fate as the civilisations of the past? I think we will, unless we change the way we produce food and fibre, and develop an environmental and ecological conscience.

Fortunately, there is a groundswell of concerned people around the world that are searching for and practising agricultural methods that are ecologically and environmentally responsible. But unless these methods are adopted on a large scale and used to restore the landscape, we will not be able to feed the ever-increasing world's population without destroying the planet itself.

To undertake this massive restoration, individual farms need to function as regenerative ecosystems and mimic the function of nature.

Convict Connections

During the 1600s and early 1700s, the inhabitants of Britain were an agrarian society with most people living in rural areas producing the bulk of their food, clothing, furniture and tools in their homes or small rural shops, using hand tools or simple machines. The Industrial Revolution, with the development of mass-production methods, and steam-powered machinery from the 1760s, changed that way of life forever and in doing so created substantial social and economic problems.

In 1701 Jethro Tull invented a mechanised seed drill that planted wheat and barley at optimum depth and in uniform rows. His remarkable invention changed the way farming was done for the next three hundred years and vastly reduced the labour required when compared to planting seed by hand.

For centuries cloth was made with handloom weaving by passing a shuttle holding the yarn slowly and awkwardly from one hand to the other. In 1733 John Kay invented and patented what was to become known as 'the flying shuttle' which enabled the weaver to be far more efficient by making twice as much cloth as they could make previously. This invention revolutionised the textile industry by dramatically reducing the cost of producing clothing and was a significant contributor to the Industrial Revolution.

These inventions and many others like them made the production of merchandise much cheaper and far less labour intensive. The outcome of this was that many jobs, especially in the textile industry, could now be done at significantly reduced wages by unskilled labourers, or even children, rather than skilled tradespeople.

Labour saving devices like Jethro Tull's seed drill had the effect of moving the population from rural areas to the cities, creating dramatic changes in lifestyle, along with harsh conditions and poverty. The machinery innovations of the Industrial Revolution had removed many people's ability to earn a wage since machines replaced many jobs. As unemployment rose, so did crime, in particular the theft of necessities such as food and clothing. In an effort to control the rapidly rising crime rate the British authorities issued very harsh penalties for minor crimes by giving jail sentences of seven years for petty theft.

As severe penalties were implemented and the prison population grew during the 18th century, the British government started to send convicts from prisons like Newgate and the county prisons to overseas penal colonies.

Initially, North America was used as the dumping ground for British convicts but the practice of transportation ended by way of the American Revolutionary War (1775-83) with America refusing to accept any more convicts.

With the loss of North America as a penal colony, alternative lodgings would be needed for the one thousand offenders convicted each year and crammed into the already overcrowded gaols of Britain. The building of jails was delayed, with the Government preferring to search for other places to send the convicts. A temporary solution was found by using old ships which were no longer seaworthy, naval or merchant ships called 'hulks' which were used to house the convicts on the River Thames.

A new dumping ground had to be found for the prisoners. The answer came with the British explorer, and Sea Captain, James Cook's voyage to the South Pacific in 1770, and the discovery of the previously uncharted continent of New Holland. Cook claimed the eastern half of the continent for Britain, naming it "New South Wales", and suggested the country would be ideal for a penal colony.

In 1787, after Captain James Cook's discovery, the British government appointed 'the eastern coast of New South Wales as the country to transport convicts, and on the 22nd January 1788, the First Fleet had arrived in Port Jackson to set up a prison colony. The fleet consisted of eleven ships containing five hundred and four male convicts, one hundred and ninety-two female convicts and fourteen children.

In 1798 the eastern half of Australia was called New South Wales and was not to be known as Australia until after 1824, when the British Admiralty officially approved the name after the New South Wales Governor, Lachlan Macquarie, recommended that the name Australia be adopted.

For the next eighty years over 160,000 men, women and children would be sent to Australia. Most of these Australian convicts were not hardened criminals but petty thieves.

Murderers and armed robbers were usually hanged rather than sentenced to life in Australia.

The transportation of convicts to Australia eventually ended in 1868 in answer to concerns that it was not a deterrent, and not a just punishment for minor crime. Also, the growing population of settlers and ex-convicts began to see themselves as 'Australians' and resented Britain dumping its most troubled people in their country.

The story of my life, and the Seis family in Australia, starts in Britain on the 18th April 1798. My great great, great, great, grandfather, seventeen-year-old William Moore, from the Parish of Hampstead, Middlesex, was in court, at the Old Bailey, London for 'stealing clothing with force of arms'. The clothing he took was one linen shirt valued at five shillings and one pair of worsted stockings valued at two shillings and sixpence. Before William's day in court he had been a farm labourer, tending sheep and cattle, and planting crops by hand. Britain in the 1790s was a country of change, the Industrial Revolution had hit Britain, and young William's life was never to be the same. He was no longer required to work on the farm because improved ploughs and seeding equipment had made his manual labour redundant and machinery replaced him. He, like many thousands of other people, became unemployed, and with no means of supporting himself, was forced to steal to survive.

In the Old Bailey court, William was proven guilty of his crime and given the sentence of seven years transportation to Port Jackson, New South Wales.

While awaiting transportation William spent two years on a filthy prison ship called a 'hulk' which was anchored on the bank of the River Thames. During the day William and hundreds of other convicts were put to forced labour on the docks, and at night the prisoners were chained to their bunks to prevent them escaping ashore.

Eventually William set sail, accompanied by three

hundred other male convicts, on the 23rd May 1800, aboard the 'Royal Admiral' and arrived one hundred and eighty-one days later on the 20th November 1800, at what would have felt like the edge of the world, in Port Jackson New South Wales. He was fortunate to survive the trip - forty-three of his fellow convicts died during the voyage. Many convicts succumbed to disease, malnutrition and scurvy during the early days of transportation, due to the poor, inadequate diet, and the very cramped, airless conditions on the ship that only measured 118 feet long and 36 feet wide.

On arrival after the dreadful trip, almost all of the prisoners including William were sick and required medical attention. William eventually recovered and was 'put to work' on public works constructing roads and later, because of his farming experience, working on the government farms.

After a few years of 'good behaviour', William was given his 'Ticket of Leave' which was a document given to convicts that granted them the freedom to work and live within a district of the colony, before their sentence expired. In 1810 he was made a free citizen when he was given his 'Certificate of Freedom', which was a document given to a convict at the end of their sentence. The certificate stated that the convict was now a free person and could seek employment, or leave the colony. William chose to stay in the colony - there was no life for him in Britain, and New South Wales was starting to give him opportunities that he could never have in 'the old country.'

As William was being given his freedom, unknown to him, on the 20th February 1811, Eleanor Wise was in the Old Bailey being convicted of stealing a gown valued at seven shillings. Eleanor, a maidservant, was given a seven-year sentence and transported to New South Wales.

After one hundred and forty-three days on the convict transport ship the *Minstrel*, Eleanor arrived in Port Jackson on 25 October 1812. All one hundred and twenty-seven women, including Eleanor, were in a fine healthy state and almost immediately put to work. At sunrise the following morning the women were taken twenty miles up the Parramatta River to the Parramatta Female Factory, which was originally a gaol built in 1796. Weaving looms were established in two upper rooms, and it became known as 'the factory above the gaol'. Eleanor and many other women were set to work, spinning and weaving wool in 'the factory' which was also to become their sleeping quarters, with many of them sleeping on the floor among the bales of wool. The significance of Eleanor being involved with wool could not have been known to her, as many of her descendants would become sheep and wool producers in the grasslands of her new country.

William Moore also worked around the Parramatta Female Factory and met Eleanor soon after her arrival. They were married at St John's Anglican Church in Parramatta, on the 12th April 1813, by the Reverend Samuel Marsden. Before she was married, Eleanor was a convict working on Government projects and the Government supplied her daily needs. Once they were married, William became responsible for Eleanor during her remaining years of conviction.

The colony was in great need of almost every occupation. Stonemasons and people with building skills were in high demand, but the most urgent need was food and the individuals with the skills to grow food. Desperate to make the colony self-sufficient, the Governor of the time started to give land grants to convicts with farming ability. Some of the early convicts with farming knowledge like James Ruse and others were allowed grants of land and had shown that crops like wheat and corn could be grown in the colony. This had given future governors the confidence to grant small farm areas to more convicts.

William had been a farm labourer before being transported to Port Jackson and because of his farming background and good behaviour he was granted fifty acres of land near the Northern Road, Castle Hill in 1819. William and Eleanor proceeded to build a home and a family of six children on the property, which they called 'Oak Hill'. On their small farm they grew wheat, corn, potatoes, and raised chickens, pigs and a few sheep, which supplied food for their family and created a small income by selling surplus produce back to the government stores. Their little farm, in what is now north western Sydney, was the start of a farming tradition in Australia that would continue until today.

Police were in short supply in the colony in the early 1800s, and convicts holding a Ticket of Leave and a record of good behaviour were sometimes appointed as police constables. In 1825 William was appointed a police constable in the district of Castle Hill and Pennant Hills. It is unbelievable to think that William, who was a convicted thief with no chance of being successful in Britain, could somehow end up as a police constable, a landowner, and respected member of the community on the other side of the world. And yet it had happened.

While William and Eleanor were making a life for themselves in fledgling Australia, in 1827 Nicholas Seis was born in the German state of Baden. No one could have known that ninety years later these two families would combine to continue and expand the Australian farming tradition.

Crossing the Mountains

In 1788 the Blue Mountains were a mountain range about 50 kilometres west of the growing convict settlement of Sydney town. Terms like 'impassable' and 'insurmountable' were used by the Governor and local authorities to describe the mountain range, to deter convicts from trying to escape in a westerly direction, from the fledgling convict settlement.

As William and Eleanor got on with their lives in the new country, the population of the settlement continued to grow as more convicts were introduced into the colony and children were being born. The increasing number of people put mounting pressure on the food supply and the area around Sydney was struggling to provide enough food for its European inhabitants. A drought in 1812 and 1813 provided the motivation to find good pasture land, so it became necessary to find a way west across the Blue Mountains. In 1813 Gregory Blaxland, William Charles Wentworth, and Lieutenant Lawson, along with, pack horses, servants and dogs set off to find a way over the mountains. After eighteen days of battling the steep terrain and avoiding deep canyons and cliffs, they succeeded in their search for a passage over the mountains, which started the agricultural expansion of Australia.

After reports of potential grazing land by Blaxland, Wentworth and Lawson, Governor Macquarie dispatched Assistant Land Surveyor George Evans to follow the trail across the Blue Mountains that had been opened by Blaxland and his companions. George Evans was to look for grassland and settlement opportunities on the western side of the newly crossed mountains. Evans, accompanied by five men, set out on the 19th of November 1813 and by the 1st December 1813, he was standing on the edge of magnificent grasslands intersected by streams and rivers. The rivers formed large ponds with abundant numbers of fish and birds of every description. The vast park-like grassland extended for miles each side of the river and expanded into the surrounding hills that had grass to their summits.

Evans was at a loss for words in relating the sight before him.

He wrote:

I am at a loss for Language to describe the Country. ...'the handsomest Country I ever saw'. The soil is exceedingly rich and produces the finest grass intermixed with variety of herbs; the hills have the look of a park; the grass here might be mowed it is so thick

and long; the farther back among these hills the better it is; the
Valleys are beautiful, as also the intervening ridges that divide
them, being thickly covered with herbage.

It should be noted that in the early 1800s, the term 'forest'
meant open woodland, and a 'plain' meant any area, whether
flat or not, that was totally or mostly devoid of trees. Thus
'forest hills' meant 'grassy hills with some trees' The
exploration conducted by Evans was of great value to the
colony. He had discovered the beautiful grassland that was to
be called the Bathurst plains and opened up a large area of
land for settlement at a time when the colony was most in
need of expansion.

In July 1814, Governor Lachlan Macquarie approved an
offer by William Cox to build a road across the Blue
Mountains, from Emu Plains west of Sydneyto the Bathurst
Plains. With the help of five free settlers, thirty convict
labourers and eight soldiers as guards, William Cox finished
the one hundred and one miles long and twelve feet wide
road in remarkably quick time, completing it in January 1815.
The crossing of the impassable mountains and the associated
road made it possible to settle the undulating and almost
treeless grasslands.

The superb, grasslands of the Bathurst Plains were created
by careful fire management and nurturing over many
thousands of years by the Indigenous Wiradjuri people.
Europeans saw this land as an excellent opportunity for the
development of agriculture, but for the Wiradjuri, it meant the
loss of their hunting grounds and the death of their ancient
culture.

In February 1818 Governor Macquarie granted ten men 50
acres of farmland each, and by 1822 there were three hundred
and forty-eight people at Bathurst, including two hundred
and eighty-four convicts, eighteen free men, fourteen free
women and thirty-three children.

With such magnificent grasslands, the settlers of the

Bathurst Plains saw an excellent opportunity to run sheep and cattle. The sheep and cattle numbers rapidly increased and within only fifty years the biologically diverse grasslands that the Wiradjuri people had nurtured for many thousands of years were showing signs of ecological decline.

GOLD

There was political unrest and associated hard times in the homeland of the Seis family in Baden, Germany, during the mid-1800s. With a sense of adventure, nineteen-year-old Nicholas Seis decided to leave his home. On the 25th of October 1845, he caught the ship *Peter Godfrey* to Melbourne, Australia.

In 1845 Melbourne was just ten years old and growing. Nicholas had worked as a butcher in Germany and secured work in a butcher shop in Melbourne until the richest goldfield the world had ever known was discovered in 1851, seventy miles north of Melbourne. The lure of gold and instant wealth changed Nicholas' mind about being a butcher, and he walked to the goldfields town of Ballarat where eventually there would be over 10,000 fellow miners from all parts of the world with the same dream of finding the precious metal.

Trouble was brewing on the goldfields. The opportunistic Government Gold Commissioner enforced a mining licence and introduced heavy-handed licence checks which were enforced by aggressive and corrupt armed police. The miners retaliated by refusing to cooperate. They burned their licences and threw rocks at the police. This then escalated into a full-scale revolt with the miners building a makeshift wooden barricade at the Eureka gold diggings. On the 3rd December 1854, the military launched an attack on the 'Eureka Stockade' overwhelming the miners, which resulted in the deaths of 22 miners and 6 soldiers. Although the battle was lost, the fight for equality was won. The miners achieved the abolition of the mining licence and a vote for all miners, but history has told us they achieved much more than that. The battle for fairness and democracy on the goldfields showed the government that it could no longer ignore the voice of popular opinion, and set Australia on a path of fairness and democracy for all Australians that continues to today.

Nicholas narrowly missed the rebellion that was to change Australia. During the lead-up to the revolt, he had become uneasy with the tension around the goldfields and the requirement to buy a miners licence, so after much backbreaking work and failing to find any gold, he pushed a self-made wooden wheelbarrow loaded with his belongings, 550 miles, to Sydney. After the long, tiring trek north, he secured a job as a butcher at Penrith on the outskirts of Sydney, but gold fever struck again. Gold had been discovered 100 miles west of Sydney, near Bathurst, and Nicholas uprooted to head to the gold fields along the Blue Mountains road that was built forty years earlier by William Cox and his team of convicts.

He was soon digging for gold again, but this time he was more fortunate and found enough gold to purchase a dray and five horses to start a carrying business. Nicholas carried goods from Sydney to the Bathurst goldfields but quickly realised that there was potential further afield. He began carting goods to the young growing towns and pastoral districts of Mudgee, Uarbry and Coolah, then headed west to Gilgandra and Coonamble where he took backloads of wool to Sydney. These trips took him through the district where the township of Gulgong was to grow out of its gold-laden soil in a few years later.

Squatters William Bowman and Richard Rouse settled in the Gulgong region in the 1820s. Rouse had vast holdings, which included the area where the town of Gulgong now stands. Richard Rouse's Shepherd, Tom Saunders, created the

Gulgong gold rush with the discovery of fourteen ounces of gold at Red Hill in 1870. Within six weeks five hundred miners had flocked to the town, and by 1872 there were 20 000 people of all nationalities and all social levels on the goldfields.

Seamen like Alexander McMillan from Scotland worked alongside local farmers, and Irish, Chinese, English and North American miners, all searching for instant wealth. Most did not find gold, but some did, with 15,000 kilograms of gold being removed from the Gulgong goldfields between 1870 and 1880.

Nicholas Seis was not interested in becoming a gold miner in Gulgong. His gold digging days were done and he was now only interested in supplying and delivering goods to the goldfield with his now thriving carrying business. He liked the lightly timbered grassland forty kilometers north of Gulgong and bought a forty-acre farm near the township of Uarbry in 1868, and four years later was able to obtain an adjoining forty acres. Nicholas immediately started to develop the small holding by planting an orchard, but because his farm consisted of only 80 acres (32 hectares), he continued to operate his carrying business.

The surveyor's report (reproduced verbatim) on Nicholas first forty acre block dated 6th February 1868 states:

> *The improvements consist of a small hut: value £5*
> *Soil of limestone formation, good, very stony in places. Timber, open forest of box, apple, and gum. There is no permanent water on this land.*

The hut on Nicholas newly purchased land had been built previously. It was very small and consisted of two rooms. One room had a fireplace with a chimney at one end and was used as a kitchen and dining area. The other room was a bedroom. The walls of the hut were built from timber, two inches thick and eight inches wide, and placed on the wall vertically. The wall timber was called slabs and made from the Indigenous ironbark eucalyptus tree by splitting the timber using steel wedges. The roof was covered with bark sheets stripped from the locally growing stringybark tree and lashed to the round timbered rafters with a rope made from bark. The floor consisted of bare earth.

The surveyor's report included the term 'open forest'. This phrase was used in the 1800s as a term to describe tree density of grassland which had a scattering of trees at a frequency of one to three trees an acre or trees about fifty meters apart. Grassland with this tree density was often described as resembling an English park which meant that Nicholas did not need to remove any of the trees from his farm to grow crops or graze sheep.

Nicholas was soon to experience his first of many Australian droughts. During 1873 most of western New South Wales went into a severe drought. All surface water vanished, including the Talbragar River, a few miles from Nicholas' farm.

In March of 1873, Nicholas was watering his horse team at a well sunk near the river when he met the girl who would be his wife. Catherine Scheimer, a shepherd's daughter from a nearby farm.

Nicholas and Catherine married the following year, on the 18th of June 1874 and soon had a growing family to feed. To help supply food for his family, Nicholas selected one acre of level ground and dug the soil with a hoe to prepare the soil for planting wheat. The seed was spread by hand, and the area levelled with a rake.

Nicholas' first crop was reasonably successful. He harvested the grain by hand and made it into flour, which Catherine then baked into bread. A vegetable garden was established as an essential part of the small farm, and it was Catherine's (Granny Seis's) job to maintain the garden for her

Nicholas & Catherine Bale

ever-growing family. Catherine, much to the amusement of everyone who saw her, had to chase the numerous 'rat kangaroos' or eastern bettongs (*Bettongia gaimardi*) out of her vegetable garden with a roughly made bush broom. Eventually, a paling fence just two feet high and made out of sticks, constructed around the area, was all that was required because the bettong was relatively small and was unable to jump any significant height. Bettongs were numerous in the 1870s, and although they caused much heartache for Granny, the creatures rarely nibbled the green leaf of the vegetables but instead ate roots and fungi.

EXPANSION

In the 1840s squatters were occupiers of grazing land held by the Crown, beyond the prescribed limits of settlement. The squatters contributed to the growth of the country's wool industry and the development of a dominant social class in Australian life. By the late 1840s, the authorities recognised the economic benefits derived from the squatters' activity and issued them leases of up to fourteen years for their sheep runs. By this time, the squatters had a hold on the land, and many had become wealthy grandees.

The 1850s saw a massive influx of immigrants, as well as thousands of miners drawn to Australia by the discovery of gold. There was a need for more land and more people on the land, so the legislative assemblies of the various colonies passed 'selection' acts in subsequent years. This act forced the squatters to bid against farmers for land that they had been living on for years. Having more money the squatters were able to purchase the best land, but much of the poorer grazing country fell into the hands of the small farmers. The squatters' hostility against the selectors and their rugged pioneer ethos led the squatters to resist social and political change.

In 1888 a grant of 1280 acres of land became available for £1 (two dollars) an acre, fifteen miles west of the original eighty-acre block. The property was commonly known as 'Round Camp', named after a shepherd's camp in a vast tract of land that was secured in 1822 by squatter William Bowman and his family. The area was regarded, as prime sheep country and Bowman placed a shepherd on 'Round Camp' to run sheep in the area. The attraction to 'Round Camp' was the lush grassland which consisted of an abundant species of grasses, forbs and herbs which was very similar to the Bathurst grasslands discovered by George Evans.

There was discontentment between the squatters and selectors during that period, with the squatter believing the selector was stealing his land and the selector knowing he had purchased the property legally. The Bowman and Seis families were no different, with the main water supply, a well, being a point of contention. One evening Nicholas' well was destroyed by unknown people tossing the nearby wooden water troughs into it and rendering it unusable.

The Bowman and Seis families ultimately resolved their differences and started a friendship which continued for generations. With these early problems behind them, Nicholas pulled down the small two-room hut on his original small farm and relocated it to Round Camp for Granny and their growing family.

Previously Nicholas and Granny obtained some merino sheep and started a breeding program, and although it was unknown to them at the time, merino sheep were to become the mainstay for the Seis family for the next 140 years.

Nicholas and Granny started to concentrate on increasing the sheep numbers, and soon Round Camp was running 600 merinos. Wheat acreage was expanded to five acres in 1889 and by 1896 not only was the wheat area increasing, but the family was also. Now there were nine children.

The family had outgrown the two-room hut, so Nicholas built a larger six room slab house with bark roof and wooden floor, a short distance from the original building.

With 1280 acres to look after, Nicholas stopped his carrying business and concentrated on running and improving the farm. By 1898 they had fenced the property, as required by law, to meet government occupancy ordinances, and had cleared ten acres of land for growing wheat. Much work was needed, and the most important was killing or 'ringbarking' the 'ever invading' trees that kept the family busy for the next fifty years. After the drought in 1870 and the inevitable run of good years following the drought, trees had germinated everywhere, encroaching and insidiously destroying the grassland.

For many thousands of years previously, Indigenous land management had maintained the grassland at very low tree densities with selective and careful fire management. The local Indigenous people were last seen and recorded by Nicholas in the late 1880s. They were a group of six men skirting around the edge of a low line of hills called Barneys Reef on the south-western side of Round Camp, hunting kangaroos and wallabies as they had done for millennia. Sadly, that was the last recorded sighting of them.

BUSHRANGERS

During the 1860s the Indigenous Wiradjuri people were not the only ones inhabiting the area in and around the sandstone hills of Barneys Reef. Gold had been discovered about forty miles from the town of Mudgee near the Talbragar River, from which the village of Denison Town emerged. As gold discoveries always do, the area attracted a diverse range of people, most of which were trying to make their fortunes honestly. A small handful wanted to earn money the easy way, by stealing. Many of these less than honest people have been recorded in Australia's history as 'bushrangers'.

During the early days of Australia's colonial development, the Chinese settlers were generally honest and law-abiding. There was only one recorded Chinese bushranger in Australia, and he was destined to inhabit the caves that are dotted along the northern escarpment of Barneys Reef, which now adjoins the Seis family properties. That person was Sam Poo, who had been a laundryman in Sydney before moving west to try his luck on the goldfields. Due to his offensive, ill-tempered, introverted manner, and his refusal to mix with either whites or Chinese, he was nicknamed 'Cranky Sam'. Sam's skill at finding gold was feeble, and he probably should have stayed a laundryman. One night he disappeared from the diggings to start his infamous handiwork.

In January 1865, ten Chinese prospectors left the Talbragar diggings and set out toward Mudgee. At a lonely spot on the road near Barneys Reef, Sam Poo bailed them up at gunpoint and robbed his countrymen of the small calico containers filled with gold dust that they had concealed under their pigtails.

Always on foot, Sam Poo continued to hold up and rob prospectors and settlers who traversed the country alone. On 8th February 1865, he attacked and raped a woman, holding her a prisoner all day and finally letting her go at nightfall, then disappearing into the darkness of Barneys Reef. Even this did not inspire the gold prospectors to leave their diggings to capture Sam Poo. On the 10th of February 1865 Trooper John Ward set out alone to arrest him. After much searching he found Sam, who upon spotting the trooper, ran for the cover and protection of the Reef. Ward rode after and finally cornered him, ordering the outlaw to drop his sawn-off shotgun. Sam Poo aimed at the trooper and fired, hitting him in the pelvic area. As Trooper Ward fell to the ground, he fired two shots from his Colt pistol at Sam Poo as he ran away through the bush. Seeing that Ward was incapable of retaliating, Sam Poo returned, took the trooper's weapons, and disappeared into the protection of Barneys Reef, leaving Ward to die from his wounds. Ward lay helpless all day and night, until noon the next day, when the local property owner found him, and he gasped the details of what occurred before whispering 'Take care of my wife and children' with his dying breath.

A widespread manhunt with armed troopers and local settlers on horseback quickly swung into action and searched for many days in vain for Sam Poo. An Indigenous tracker named Harry Hughes volunteered his services, quickly picked up the trail and led the troopers to a location a few miles away, where they found the Chinese bushranger. Sam Poo was not going to be captured quickly, and a running gun battle ensued for several hours. Trooper Todd finally shot Sam Poo in the thigh, but the outlaw continued firing while shot and lying on the ground. They rushed him and, showing no mercy, clubbed the bushranger with a rifle butt, breaking the stock and fracturing Sam Poo's skull.

Critically wounded, Sam Poo was taken to Mudgee Hospital, where he eventually recovered from his injuries. When he was fit to travel Sam Poo was taken on the 70-mile journey to Bathurst Gaol where he was hanged on 19th December 1865, after being found guilty of Trooper Ward's murder.

Sam Poo was not the only Bushranger to haunt the area where the Seis family would settle a few years later. One such man, called 'Heather', occasionally worked as a sawyer in the timber trade, and a bullock driver, but his primary occupation was a bushranger who frequented the Barneys Reef area, robbing from the local squatters and gold prospectors travelling the road that passed over the western side of the reef.

Following is an extract from the Mudgee Newspaper 'The Western Post', April 7th, 1863

A BUSHRANGER SHOT DEAD

On Saturday, intelligence reached Mudgee that Mr. Robert Lowe, who was travelling in a buggy on the Talbragar road, accompanied by a man on horseback, had been stuck-up by two bushrangers, who had the last few days been successfully carrying on their depredations in the neighbourhood of Slapdash. Mr. Lowe, on being ordered to stand, was covered with a revolver, and commanded with a threat to get out of his buggy; seeing that the determined villain was bent upon mischief, he quickly levelled a gun he happened to have with him, the contents of which he lodged in the fellow's neck and breast, which proved fatal. Mr. Lowe at once despatched a messenger to Mr. War- burton, P.M., who sent the police with a conveyance for the body. The police upon reaching the spot, found that some parties had buried the body between two pieces of bark; it was exhumed, and brought into Mudgee, where it was identified as that of a man who had worked as a sawyer, and occasionally drove a team of bullocks for a person engaged in the timber trade

The spate of robberies, murder and rape happening around the district was very concerning to Nicholas and Granny, as well as to the whole district. The story of the bushrangers has morphed into local legend with Granny Seis telling the stories to her grandson Harry, and Harry retelling the story to his family, and on to me. There were very few other incidents like these until Jimmy Governor went on a murderous rampage on the 20th of July 1900...but that is another story.

· · ·

GRASSLANDS

While the Indigenous fire management kept the grassland healthy and species-rich, the little marsupial bettong that gave Granny much heartache with her vegetable patch was maintaining and improving the soil. During the late 1800 bettongs were in large numbers and aerated the soil while digging for underground fungi or truffles. This action distributed fungi and microorganisms throughout the grassland soil. The aeration by bettongs allowed better water infiltration, and the distribution of soil microorganisms created ideal soil.

The property was running six hundred sheep without difficulty because of the excellent grassland, so Nicholas and Granny decided to increase the number of sheep on the farm. Before that could be done, it became necessary to fence and subdivide the farm to better manage them, so a fencing program was started. This required the hard work of cutting trees, splitting posts, digging holes and running wire.

The family continued to grow as more children were born. With the increasing family numbers also came a workforce. All the children were expected to help with the jobs like fencing, clearing timber and feeding the horse team.

Even though the work of ring-barking trees, fencing and running increasing numbers of merino sheep was hard work, financially things were going well. With increasing financial security, in November 1899 Nicholas decided to buy a new three horse dray to replace the now worn out five horse wagon that was used for the last twenty-nine years in his cartage business. Nicholas harnessed the horse team onto the wagon and loaded it with wool from the 600 recently shorn sheep and, with Granny, headed on the twenty-mile journey to Gulgong. While in Gulgong they sold their wool, bought Christmas presents for the nine children, purchased the new dray and started the journey toward home. Five miles short of their home, near the property called Slapdash, the horses bolted, throwing Nicholas, Granny, and Christmas presents to the ground. Granny and presents were unhurt, but Nicholas fell under the dray and was seriously injured with a broken leg. Granny recovered the horses and dray, loaded Nicholas and the presents, and headed to Gulgong Hospital. Nicholas experienced medical complications during his extended stay in the hospital, and unfortunately, his leg required amputation.

The implications of Nicholas having his leg amputated were devastating for the family; he could no longer do everyday farming tasks such as ploughing and ringbarking. Even the usually simple task of climbing on a wagon was almost impossible. Fortunately, Granny, being born into a farming family, readily adopted the role of running the farm. With the help of the oldest son Joseph who was sixteen, and William aged twelve, Granny did the ploughing, ringbarking, harnessing horse teams and general farm work. Nicholas switched roles with Granny, looking after the young children and cooking the meals. Nicholas, who previously was a tailor as well as a butcher, made clothes for the whole family. The children wore clothes made from flour bags, and Granny's flour bag undies were often seen hanging on the clothesline.

Things were going well with Granny and the older children running the farm. These were good financial times for the Seis family, until disaster struck in the form of the horrendous Federation drought.

CATHERINE (GRANNY SEIS)

Catherine, having been born in Germany, arrived in Australia in 1855 as a three-year-old child, with her parents Joseph and Eva Schiemer

Members of the Schiemer family had been shepherds for generations, and when the family arrived in the district Joseph was given a job as a shepherd at the extensive nearby property, Tongy Station, which had been granted to former convict Richard Fitzgerald.

Catherine was the first born in the family and spent much of her time with her father tending sheep. As well as gaining invaluable knowledge with the management of sheep, she also acquired skills in the management of the grasslands of the new colony of Australia. This early experience would be a great asset in the future for her and future generations.

Granny's childhood experience would also be a turning point in the family when she took over the role of running Roundcamp. Being female, she instilled a nurturing ethos onto William and Joseph and later to her grandson Harry.

At the age of nine, Harry became seriously ill with acute rheumatic fever, and typical of Granny's beautiful nature she nursed him back to health. Harry was sick for many months, and it was during this time in the evenings in front of the open fire with Granny smoking her old pipe, that she instilled a great love of animals and agriculture in his young mind. She told him in great detail about sheep, and horses, but equally importantly she told him about how she and Nicholas ran the farm and spoke about the grasslands and trees. She also described how they managed the drought of the late 1870s and the Federation drought of the early twentieth century.

One of her more enlightening pieces of information was the very rapid invasion of trees that grew like weeds and altered the grasslands, after the wet years of the early 1880s.

The time spent with Granny was most likely the best education anyone of that era could have had, and it influenced Harry by teaching a nurturing ethic of animals and the land which would be passed down to future generations.

BLOW-FLIES, DROUGHT AND RABBITS

Many animals like the cane toad, rabbit and fox have been introduced into Australia with disastrous economic and environmental consequences, but one of the worst introductions has been an insignificant looking blue-green fly. Lucilia cuprina, the Australian sheep blowfly, is oddly named as it originated from South Africa and arrived in Australia an uninvited guest as a stowaway on sheep from South Africa in about 1880.

The introduction of the blowfly coincided with another introduction in the 1880s. Merino rams were imported into Australia from Vermont in the USA. The Australian stud merino breeders of that time believed that the Vermont sheep would improve Australia's sheep flock by increasing wool cuts. With the use of some smart marketing, the sheep spread rapidly around Australia. Although the fleece weight was high, the clean yield of the wool was low, and of poor quality, the sheep were also covered with excessive skin wrinkle which increased the risk of fly strike. The wool on the Vermont sheep was short, very dense and carried excessive amounts of grease and oil. This was the ideal environment for the newly introduced blowfly to lay her eggs. The importers and promoters of the new Vermont sheep could not have foreseen the fly menace because the Australian native flies did not cause any problems with sheep and Nicholas Seis did not report any fly blown sheep in his flock until after 1900.

The wrinkly Vermont sheep craze was destined for a short life, with Mother Nature solving the problem by way of drought. The Vermont sheep were originally bred in a very lush environment, and consequently were not bred for hardiness and a good constitution.

The years between 1895 and 1902 were a period of record low rainfall that affected most of Australia and became known as the Federation Drought. It was Australia wide and when it finally broke in 1902, the total sheep population had halved to fewer than 54 million, from a total of 106 million in 1891. Meanwhile cattle numbers had fallen by more than forty percent.

Many of the dead sheep were the poorly constituted Vermont-bred sheep that were not suitable to Australia's climatic conditions, and most could not survive such a long drought. The drought and Vermont sheep left a dreadful legacy. The sheep blowfly had millions of dead sheep carcases to breed on during the seven years of drought, and their numbers increased to the billions that would continue to devastate the Australian sheep industry for the next one hundred years.

Nicholas and Granny did not pursue the wrinkly Vermont craze and kept breeding their plain bodied Tasmanian blood sheep during this era. But the drought was so severe that their dams completely dried up, and with no ability to cart water, four hundred of their six hundred sheep died of thirst.

Even though they saved two hundred sheep, they could not escape the menace of the increasing numbers of blowflies that would continue to worry the next four generations of the Seis family.

These years were an extremely worrying and depressing time for Nicholas and Granny. Not only did they lose over half of their sheep, but all of their wheat crops failed as well.

As with many droughts, it broke with a magnificent season in 1903. With the help of good rainfall and a new variety of wheat called 'Federation', the family grew one hundred acres of wheat which yielded an unheard of 15 bags per acre (almost 3 tonnes per hectare), and the sale of the wheat paid the debt that had accumulated during the drought years.

Since wheat was first grown in Australia until the 1960s, wheat yield has been measured in bags per acre. A bag of wheat contains three bushels and weighs one hundred and eighty pounds or almost eighty-two kilograms.

Today wheat yield is measured in tonnes per hectare. E.g.: 12 bags per acre is approximately one tonne per acre or 2.4 tonnes per hectare.

Rabbits

In 1904 there was great excitement from eight-year-old Henry. He had discovered a strange looking, furry, four-legged animal. None of the children knew what it was or how it was about to change their lives. It was a rabbit, an animal introduced from Britain. In a few years, thousands of European wild rabbits would move in from the west as if in a line and devastate everything in their path.

Within ten years most of the grassland had been destroyed, not only because rabbits ate the grass but also because they dug it up and ate the roots. With rabbits consuming all of the grass, the sheep had nothing to eat. The voracious appetite of the newcomers not only created great hardship for everyone, but it also started the soil eroding. With the soil now having no protection from grass cover, it was exposed to the elements of rain and wind. This combination of bare soil, wind and rain created significant soil erosion. Topsoil blew away, and huge gullies appeared, depositing eroded soil into the rivers. The combination of rabbits and soil erosion devastated the countryside and filled the rivers with silt in the 1920s. The land and rivers have never fully recovered.

The amount of topsoil that was lost during that period will never be known. The massive soil loss included nutrients and soil carbon that took thousands of years for the grasslands to create.

Unfortunately, the rabbits destroyed the grassland that sustained the bettongs, which could not compete with them. The rabbits were the death knoll of the bettongs, and the last one was seen around 1906. The small marsupial that kept the soil and grassland healthy was gone forever.

Rabbits created very hard times by decimating crops and pasture which restricted the numbers of sheep and cattle that could be run. In spite of this, the rabbits became a source of food and income, with many people trapping rabbits and selling the skins for three shillings a pound (approximately sixty cents a kilogram).

With the use of rabbit-proof netting to fence paddocks and allow rabbit eradication programs, wheat growing and wool production were able to continue.

Another source of income was koala skins. The shooting of koalas for their skin is rarely spoken about today, but during the early 1900s, Koala fur was sold and made into coats and hats. The skins were a valuable income source for the family until the koalas were reduced to such low numbers that today, sadly, there are no koalas in the district.

Depressed wool prices created tough financial times during the first decade of the 1900s. At the outbreak of World War I prices improved considerably, due to the demand for woolen service uniforms.

The price of wool was almost 60 percent higher in 1920 than in 1903. These excellent wool prices were sustained for ten years which enabled the family to purchase an adjoining area of 1100 acres (458 hectares). This additional land allowed them to increase sheep numbers, and by 1920 they were running over 2000 sheep and four head of cattle. In 1922 the wool from their 2000 sheep was sold for £240 ($480) which was much more than the wool clip of twenty years previously.

At twenty-four years old in 1907 Joseph, (also known as young Nick) the eldest son of Nicholas and Granny, expanded the families land holdings with the purchase of a 1200-acre (500 hectares) property six miles south of Round Camp which he called 'Rosevale'. By 1925 Joseph was running 1200 Tasmanian blood merino sheep and five head of cattle.

The combining of two very different families happened in 1911 when my grandfather Joseph married Elizabeth McMillan and had three boys, Harry (my father), Alec and Keith. Elizabeth was a daughter of Mary Anne Ashby, granddaughter of the convicts William Moore and Eleanor Wise, who arrived in Port Jackson in the early 1800s and ran their small farm near Castle Hill, in north-west Sydney.

Most people were ashamed of their convict ancestors, and Mary Anne (my great grandmother) was not proud of her convict lineage; she never mentioned it and hid her family connections from everyone. This was not unusual at this time, with many Australian families discovering their convict heritage only in recent times.

Elizabeth's father was a Scottish seaman, Alexander McMillan, who after the ship docked at Newcastle Harbour, jumped ship and headed to the Gulgong goldfields. Alexander and Mary Anne arrived in Gulgong as the gold rush was starting and were some of the very first residents of the rapidly growing town.

Elizabeth started a family tradition that was passed down from her Scottish heritage: no work on Sundays. Many of these days were spent playing tennis at Round Camp and neighbouring properties. The other outing was fishing on the

Talbragar River, only a few miles from Rosevale. During the early 1900s, the Talbragar was a beautiful river with massive river red gum and casuarina trees along its banks, which shaded the deep permanent waterholes. The water in the river and waterholes was clear, which enabled the sighting of many fish on the gravel riverbed. On Sundays, Joseph and Elizabeth would often take the boys fishing. While Joseph and the older boys hitched the horse and sulky, Elizabeth prepared picnic lunch. Mum, Dad and the three kids would eagerly climb into the sulky and travel seven miles to the Talbragar River. Not only were these days fun for the family, but they were also very productive, catching cod, yellow belly and silver perch, which provided Sunday night dinner at Round Camp with the ageing Granny and Nicholas.

These fishing trips were short lived. The thousands of rabbits plus the increasing numbers of sheep and cattle caused major soil erosion around much of eastern Australia, and the Gulgong area was not spared. The mud-laden water running into the Talbragar River after heavy rain caused silting, and the muddy oxygen-depleted water killed the fish and filled the waterholes.

The fish have never returned to the numbers of pre-1920, and there are very few fish in the Talbragar River today.

The good financial times continued into the 1920s. Much to Granny's disgust, in 1925 Joseph purchased a brand new T model Ford. The older generation of the time hated motor cars because they were noisy and smelly, but mostly because horses were terrified of them, and would frequently bolt in panic, sometimes killing or harming the horse and causing severe injuries to riders and passengers.

Joseph was not to be deterred by Granny's negative comments, and the car salesman arrived with the shiny new Ford car. Joseph, who had never driven a car before, was given lessons by the car salesman. Like most young males, he didn't listen to the instructions. Mum, Dad and kids climbed into the shiny new contraption and full of confidence headed down the dirt road. Within a few hundred yards Joseph tried to negotiate the first right-hand corner by pulling on the steering wheel as one would pull on the reins of a horse, failed to take the bend, and crashed the car. Fortunately, the only thing injured was Joseph's pride. His driving skill did not improve much; years later he crashed the car again, on the very last day that he drove the vehicle.

The kids' fun did not end with the fishing and T model car trips. The three boys travelled ten miles by horse and sulky to a bark-hut school. Being young boys, they hated school but loved the trip home. The Seis family horse was a thoroughbred cross draught horse which was an excellent, fast sulky horse. The kids from the neighbouring farm also had a fast horse, and of course the inevitable happened: a race home most afternoons after school. This great fun lasted for months until Joseph noticed the exhausted horse and put a stop to it.

In 1920 Nicholas, at age ninety-four and Granny aged sixty-nine, decided to retire from farm work and bought a house in Gulgong, leaving William and Henry to run the farm.

In October 1922, at age ninety-six, Nicholas died, and Granny continued to live in Gulgong until her death in 1936 aged eighty-four. The passing of Nicholas and Granny saw the end of an era in the Seis family, but memories of Granny, the grand family matriarch, sitting in front of the open fire smoking her pipe, are still shared by her descendants today. Granny left a great impression on her eldest grandson Harry, who learned a great deal from her and spoke very fondly of his grandmother even as an old man in his eighties.

THE START OF INDUSTRIALIZED AGRICULTURE

As a fifteen-year-old in 1928, my father Harry was trapping rabbits on a neighbouring 1100 acre (460 hectares) property. It was a hot, dusty day, so he went looking for water and found a spring on the western boundary. After filling his hat and drinking from it, he spat out the foul-tasting water. It was salty. Harry did not realise the significance of the discovery of saline water as a fifteen-year-old, but it was to have severe consequences for the property of Winona in the future.

One year later Harry leased Winona, which had been part of the original Merotherie estate that had been squatted by William Bowman in 1822. Like most of the country in the District, Winona had lightly timbered grassland before 1870. The original selector's deeds, dated the 29th of January 1904, indicated that the tree invasion had already started. The documents describe thickly timbered ironbark and stringybark saplings in most areas of the property. (*Saplings are trees up to 15-20 years old*). A lot of the trees were already ringbarked, and small areas were cleared of trees when Harry leased it, so as well as running 700 merino sheep he decided to grow small areas of wheat.

Harry's father Joseph had never enjoyed growing wheat, or the work involved in preparing the horses for work. He said that you had to get up in the dark very early in the morning to feed them, harness them, hook them to the plough and work behind them all day. Then detach them from the plough, remove the harness and feed them in the dark at night. His favourite saying was: 'We grow wheat so that we can feed the horses, so we can grow wheat to feed the horses.'

Not much has changed today: We grow wheat to buy inputs such as fertiliser, pesticides and diesel so we can grow wheat to buy inputs such as fertiliser, pesticides and diesel.

Not deterred by his father's dislike of growing wheat, in January 1928 Harry borrowed his father's horse team and plough to prepare a forty acre paddock for sowing with wheat in April that year. The small wheat crop yielded a respectable four bags to the acre, but Harry knew he could do better. Harry did what he would do for most of his life; he sowed his next crop differently.

Crops grown pre-1930 were sown without any fertiliser except the very occasional application of horse or cow manure. Harry had heard about a chemical fertiliser called 'New Manure' and thought he would try it with his crop. This new fertiliser, now called superphosphate, is a synthetic fertiliser that supplies the nutrients phosphorus, sulphur and calcium.

The use of the superphosphate greatly concerned Harry's father, who said it would poison the ground. In hindsight, seventy years later, his father may have been correct. Harry, however, proved he could improve wheat yields, and his one hundred acre crop produced eight bags per acre, which was double the yield of his father's crop.

Encouraged by the high wheat yields, and low wool prices, his cropping area increased to two hundred acres. This was becoming too large an area for horse teams, and Harry wanted to extend his cropping area further. He decided to become mechanised with the purchase of a new steel-wheeled Fordson tractor, a Sundercut disc plough, a seed drill, and a Sunshine Harvester. The total cost of these implements was £660 ($1320.)

Encouraged by his early success with superphosphate, Harry sowed two hundred and thirty acres in 1934, which produced a massive crop for the era, and yielded thirteen bags to the acre (2.5 tonnes per hectare) of grain. With three thousand bags of wheat to sell at one and sixpence halfpenny per bushel (or £3 per ton), he grossed £750 ($1500) for his annual crop. The high yielding wheat crops enabled Harry to purchase Winona outright in 1936 for two pounds, twelve shillings and six pence per acre (approx $5 per acre).

Harry was never happy with the steel wheeled Fordson tractor because it caused soil erosion where the wheel dug into the soil. It was also very rough to ride, and he thought it not much of an improvement on the horse teams. In 1937 he purchased a new rubber-tyred Twin City tractor for £225 ($450). With his new, more efficient tractor, the wheat area expanded to three hundred acres annually, and with the ongoing use of superphosphate, wheat growing was very profitable.

In the 1930s superphosphate cost approximately $5 per tone and wheat sold for $6 per tonne (the actual figure was one and sixpence halfpenny a bushel or about 3 pounds per tonne).

Growing wheat was much more profitable in the 1930s than today. Today superphosphate is over $300 per tonne and wheat averages $150-200 per tonne. We would need to be getting over $300 per tonne for wheat growing today to be equal.

In 1935 it took seventy-five tonnes of wheat to purchase a new tractor. In 2018 it would take over five hundred tonnes.

With relatively low production costs and good yields the area sown to wheat expanded over Australia during 1930 to 1940. Harry's high yielding crops were grown with minimal inputs of about thirty pounds per acre (30 kilogram per hectare) of superphosphate, and there was no herbicide, or pesticide used in that era. Today world agriculture uses enormous amounts of fertiliser, herbicides and fungicides to achieve yields not much better than what my father produced in the 1930's.

By the mid-1940s, Winona had now been ploughed, cultivated and sown to wheat for seventeen years without rest. Very few original perennial grass species remained. The combination of these factors caused soil structure to decline. Paddocks were hard and compacted, and soil carbon was severely depleted to an estimated half percent from around five percent of the original grassland soil.

Within ten years Harry was starting to see a decline in crop yields. Not knowing the reasons for the lower yields, and with good wheat prices because of the war in Europe, he continued growing three hundred acres (125 hectares) of wheat on Winona annually and running seven hundred sheep.

It is now known that the combination of compacted, oxygen-depleted soil, with low soil carbon, severely depleted the soil of micro-organisms. This stopped soil nutrient cycling, prevented rainfall infiltrating into the ground, and caused wheat yields to drop dramatically.

Wheat growing had to stop, but what could be done instead? After twenty years of growing crops, there was no pasture left for the sheep. In January 1946 a very severe storm hit Winona. Significant amounts of water rushed through the loosely ploughed soil and washed enormous gullies through the length of the property. It worried Harry considerably to see Winona washing into the Talbragar River and seeing the gullies up to ten feet deep destroying the property.

It also concerned him that the native grassland species had been killed and replaced by inferior weed species after the years of wheat growing.

There was no known way that he could restore the original native grassland. In the 1940s Harry heard about methods of improving pasture, and he started experimenting with plants that were introduced into Australia from the northern hemisphere. He began sowing subterranean clover and ryegrass but found they were no more productive than the already depleted native pastures. A few years later, after a crop of wheat was sown into a subterranean clover paddock, Harry observed a significant increase in the growth and production of the clover. He reasoned that it was responding to superphosphate that was applied to the crop.

Harry was not the only person to discover that superphosphate would stimulate subterranean clover to grow to almost double its size in the phosphorus depleted Australian soil. This discovery would create an unprecedented demand for superphosphate fertiliser.

The 'sub-super' phase had begun.

THE 1940s
Mari Williams lived south of Newcastle in the lovely

fishing village of 'Cams Warf'. Destiny would have it that one day in 1937 she decided to visit a friend in Gulgong. During that visit, she met Harry Seis. You could almost say that she never left Gulgong because one year later on the 10th of June they were married and Mari stayed until her death, building a marriage across sixty years.

Harry did not own a house and was still living with his father and brothers in the house that Joseph had built many years previously. Having decided that he must have a house for his new bride, he made a two bedroom home from native cypress pine that grew on Winona. Times were tough in the 1940s, and amenities like electricity and telephone were luxuries that were not available in country New South Wales, with kerosene lamps usually supplying lighting for households. Upon hearing of a better method, Harry set an electric generating system with a petrol motor generating power and a bank of batteries to store it. This was not unlike the modern systems available now that generate power from solar panels and store the energy in batteries for use at night.

On the 28th of December 1939, a dry storm emerged from the west and bombarded the ground and set trees alight with numerous lightning strikes. With no rain to dampen the smouldering trees and strong winds blowing from the north-west, the inevitable happened. Fire emerged from one of the lightning strikes and raced toward the newly constructed house. Fortunately, Harry had the tractor attached to the disc plough and was able to create a firebreak around the house which narrowly saved it from burning.

The rabbits which had been a curse for the last thirty years had kept the grass very short around the whole district, including the area around the house, and had prevented the fire from becoming too large. No one knew that this fire was to be the forerunner of something far more severe exactly forty years later.

The 1940s were years of expansion for the newlywed

couple. After the house was built a three stand woolshed to shear Harry's increasing sheep flock was constructed, but the 1940s were more about kids. Children were soon on the way with Barry being born first, then Ian, Helen and lastly me. Harry and Mari had a problem. There were no schools close by. Gulgong School was fourteen miles away, and school buses were only used in cities. During the 1940s rural areas had one-teacher bush schools dotted about the countryside and children still travelled to school on horseback, just as their parents and grandparents did. The closest school to Winona was six miles (ten kilometres) away at a locality called Talbragar. My brother Barry owned a small pushbike, and the only way that five-year-old Barry could get any schooling was to ride his bike six miles to a cousin's home and stay there during the week while attending the nearby school. After attending school during the week, he would ride his bike six miles home for the weekend.

This arrangement did not satisfy Harry, so he decided to start a bus run for the growing number of children in the district. During those times there were no buses available, so Harry chose to build his own, which was destined to be the first school bus in country New South Wales. The bus that Harry and his neighbours created certainly would not pass regulations today. It resembled a cattle truck; in fact, it was a cattle truck. A two-ton second-hand Dodge truck with the tray area of the vehicle enclosed to resemble a primitive caravan with a door in the back and old church pews for seats. The old bus/truck was used for many years. I have great memories of my first exciting day of school, travelling in the old green bus. Eventually a real bus was purchased and the school bus run that Harry started almost 70 years ago is still used to send my grandchildren to school. But the modern school bus just doesn't have the character of the old Dodge truck.

. . .

INNOVATION

To reduce the work and time involved with ploughing, in 1945 Harry trialled something extraordinary. In late February he decided to try sowing oats directly into the grazed stubble of the previous year's wheat crop without ploughing the soil first. His aim was to sow oats for sheep feed as cheaply and efficiently as possible. His first attempt at what is now known as 'zero tilling' was a success, producing an oat crop at very low cost that he could graze with his sheep. What Harry had done was fifty years ahead of his time.

Unbeknownst to Harry, he could have been one of the very first people in the world to zero till crops. Harry persisted with this method of sowing low-cost sheep feed until annual weeds like silver grass and cape weed started to invade the crop. Because herbicides were not yet developed, Harry had no practical method of controlling weeds and was forced to stop using his unique crop sowing method and reverted to ploughing and cultivating.

Weeds had been introduced into Australia as alien plants hidden as seeds in imported food, packing materials, ship ballast, ornamental garden plants, and in seed for sowing crops. Up until the late 1940s, weeds were not a problem for Harry but twenty years of creating the perfect environment of bare uncovered soil to grow wheat had finally caught up. The introduced plants were thriving. It was unfortunate that the weeds invaded and defeated Harry's innovative zero-till cropping method because Harry had unknowingly foreseen a technique of growing crops that were to revolutionise agriculture around the world fifty years later.

THE GREEN REVOLUTION

After World War Two, agriculture was changing around the world, and Australia was no exception. Industrialised farming was being fast-tracked. The use of chemical fertiliser and pesticides was seen as the future of agriculture. Harry saw many aspects of the new agricultural revolution as very beneficial, and he became a leader in the application of modern, scientific farming methods.

Adding substances to soil to improve the growth of plants has been used for thousands of years. The Egyptians, Greeks and Romans discovered that plant growth could be improved by spreading animal manure throughout the soil. They are also known to have added seashells, clay, vegetable waste and ashes from burned weeds to the soil before growing wheat.

Diseases in crop plants have been a problem since ancient times. Rusts, blights, mildews and smuts were familiar to Hebrews, Greeks, Chinese, Indians and Romans. The Romans also were aware of lower wheat yields when red spots of rust appeared on plants. To combat the rust problem and its effects on crop yields, the Romans created a god of rust, Robigus, honoured in an annual religious ceremony for over 1700 years. During the following two millennia, little was added to the knowledge of plant diseases until the invention of the microscope in the 1600s led to the discovery of fungi and bacteria. It was not until 1802 that sulphur, applied as a finely ground dust, was used agriculturally to control mildew on fruit trees.

Research into fertiliser technology started in the early seventeenth century with the beneficial effects of saltpetre. Scientists Francis Bacon and Johann Glauber, seeing the beneficial effects of the use of saltpetre (potassium nitrate), which was used by Chinese alchemists as an oxidising agent for making gunpowder in the 9th Century. Glauber developed the first mineral fertiliser, which was a mixture of saltpetre, lime, phosphoric acid, nitrogen, and potash.

Justus von Liebig was a German chemist who is credited as the founder of agricultural chemistry and forefather of modern agriculture. In the mid-nineteenth century, he studied the importance of minerals and atmospheric nitrogen to nourish plants, resulting in his famous Law of the Minimum, which states that a deficiency in any growth-limiting factor (nutrients as well as water, light, etc.) will impair plant development.

As with fertilisers, naturally occurring pesticides have been used since ancient times. The Romans used arsenic as a method of controlling insects, and in the 16th century, Chinese farmers used nicotine as an insecticide. Insecticide development was continued in the 1930s by a group of German chemists. Organophosphate compounds were originally developed as potential chemical warfare agents and were kept secret during World War Two. After the war, these very potent compounds were introduced into industrialised agriculture as insecticides, and many organophosphate insecticides continue to be used today.

Copper and sulphur were the main fungal disease control products until the first synthetic fungicides (nabam, thiram, and zineb) were developed and patented in the 1930s. During the 1940s, agricultural experiment stations were assigned to improve disease control methods and reduce preventable crop disease losses.

DDT (dichlorodiphenyltrichloroethane) was first synthesised in 1877, but it was not until 1940 that a Swiss chemist, Dr Paul Müller, discovered that it was a very effective insecticide. It was introduced into widespread use during World War Two and became the single most important pesticide responsible for maintaining human health, mainly through the control of mosquitoes during the next two decades.

Most herbicides, or weed killers, were developed after World War Two. In 1946, the first commercially available chlorine-based herbicides were marketed to control broadleaf plants. These herbicides include 2,4-D (2,4 Dichlorophenoxyacetic acid) and 2,4,5-T (2,4,5-Trichlorophenoxyacetic acid).

Farmers in the 1950s were amazed at the effectiveness of these weed killers. With the low cost of 2,4-D, it became the first successful selective herbicide, which allowed for significantly improved weed control in wheat, corn and similar cereal grass crops, because it kills broadleaf plants, but not the crop or most grasses. This herbicide continues to be used today, and it remains one of the most commonly used herbicides in the world.

Even though many chemical fertilisers were developed in the nineteenth century and pesticides developed in the 1930s and 1940s, the history of modern industrialised agriculture began after World War Two with what is now called the Green Revolution. After the war, many people including politicians were very concerned about the growing world population and the need to feed vast numbers into the future.

The name 'Green Revolution' is credited to the work of American plant breeder Norman Borlaug, who developed high-yielding varieties of cereal grains and encouraged the expansion of irrigation infrastructure and the use of hybridised seeds, synthetic fertilisers and pesticides to farmers from the 1950s to the 1980s. The work of Norman Borlaug and others was adopted around the world with outstanding results. As the 'Green Revolution' transformed global agriculture, world grain production increased by 250 percent. It appeared that agriculture would be able to feed the growing world human population easily. Food security was achieved for many countries with the use of the new wheat, maize and rice varieties, reliant on new fertilisers, insecticides and fungicides.

The golden age of pesticides began in the 1950s. During that time, new and amazing products were being developed; they were tested mainly for their ability to kill plants, insects and plant disease-causing fungi, with very little concern for their safety. In these early days, few people thought there were downsides to pesticides. The new agricultural system was making agriculture easier as well as food cheaper and more accessible, and there were no documented cases of people dying from their regular use.

Several synthetic chemical fungicides that were developed between 1950 and 1970 proved to be effective in controlling a broad range of plant disease-causing organisms. The introduction of synthetic chemical fungicides in the 1940s led to their rapid adoption because they were more efficient in managing the fungi, did less damage to the crops, and could be used at significantly lower use rates than copper and sulphur.

The new pesticides were a wonder of science, reducing the need to weed fields by hand and reducing the need for tillage for weed control. Insects seemed to be no longer a problem; the miracle insecticide called DDT killed insects at very low cost and increased crop production by removing the threat of insect damage. We could at last feed the world easily and cheaply with no perceived downside to the excellent products that science had produced for us.

At last farmers would be free of the problems of weeds, insects, crop disease and low yields, the new products promised an increase in profit of up to 500 percent. With those potential benefits and the ease of growing crops, the adoption of chemical farming was dramatic. Between 1945 and 1972 the total expenditures on pesticides increased tenfold and the worldwide use of pesticides and fertiliser increased by many millions of kilograms during that time.

The adoption of chemical farming was so successful that chemical companies increased their production to almost 10 000 new pesticide products between 1947 and 1952 in the USA alone. This increase in the adoption of chemical farming saw that by 2012, the world was using over 2.5 billion kilograms of pesticides and the global market of crop protection products, has forecast revenues of over $52 billion US in 2019.

It appeared as though the Green Revolution had been a

great success. Has it solved the food problems of the world by producing vast amounts of food for the growing population of the world? Or has it created issues with even more significant problems looming in the future?

GREEN PASTURES, SHEEP, AND WHEAT

Harry adopted much of the Green Revolution thinking and methods with the use of new wheat and pasture varieties that were complemented with the addition of fertiliser. Insects such as red-legged earth mite and blue oat mite that can decimate crops and pastures were controlled with insecticides like DDT.

From 1950 to 1970 the whole of Winona, which by 1970 had grown to 4000 acres, was sown to sub clover and annually fertilised with one hundred and twelve pounds per acre (125 kilograms per hectare) of superphosphate.

The cost of superphosphate in the early 1950s was three pounds, two shillings and sixpence a tonne (approximately $6.25 per tonne) and with wool prices peaking at over $30 per kilogram and averaging over $10 per kilogram) it was very economical to use large quantities of the fertiliser. Some paddocks on Winona would have up to 4 tonnes per acre applied to them over the next thirty years.

Growing introduced pasture with the use of artificial fertiliser is common now, but in the 1940s and 1950s, it was regarded as very radical and innovative. Despite criticism, Harry continued to transform the degraded property with an annual application of superphosphate and the establishment of introduced pasture.

This innovative farmer fixed the erosion problems and then modified his cropping methods. He changed to using a much shorter fallow period when the paddock is ploughed before the crop was sown, by reducing the fallow period to three months from the recommended six to eight months.

This managed much of the soil erosion and produced an extra three to four months sheep grazing time, from the paddock.

This property management worked well. Winona became a highly productive property because his methods tripled the number of sheep Harry was able to run on Winona from one sheep per acre (2.4 sheep per hectare) to three sheep per acre (7.2 sheep per hectare). Even though Harry did well financially from growing wheat, his primary interest and love were merinos. In 1939 he took his first sheep (two ewes) to the local Gulgong show and won two first prizes. This success started a sheep showing tradition that has continued to the present day.

Harry wanted his sheep to be bigger and to grow more wool. He introduced new genetics into the small framed, traditional, Tasmanian blood superfine sheep that were initially bred by his grandparents Nicholas and Granny.

This break from tradition caused concern among older members of the family. Harry's father Joseph was especially critical of his decision, but undeterred by the criticism, and most likely stimulated by it, Harry was determined to breed the best sheep in the district. Armed with his new breed of big sheep with heavy fleeces, Harry exhibited at all of the local shows in the flock classes or amateur sections and beat all competitors until the other sheep producers objected and banned him from showing his sheep in the flock sections. Of course, that did not stop him. He would show his sheep in the open section, for breeders of stud sheep.

In 1949 Harry registered his Stud as 'Winona' and continued to show his sheep, again beating all comers. The following year, an outstanding ram that Harry named Bill was born on Winona. In 1952 Bill was shown at the Sydney Sheep Show and won Champion Ram. Bill was again shown in Sydney in 1954 and again was awarded Champion Ram. Bill and his sons and daughters went on to be the foundation of the Winona merino stud that we have today.

HARRY ALSO CONCENTRATED ON GROWING BETTER WHEAT CROPS and using the best science of the time purchased the latest wheat varieties with the aim of producing the very best crops. With these new types and using the most modern fertiliser, he fine-tuned wheat growing to a point where he was producing award-winning wheat crops that yielded the unheard of twenty-two bags to the acre (four tonnes per hectare).

Harry continued to improve Winona by following the best science available at the time. He planted the very latest varieties of introduced clover and grass species like perennial ryegrass and phalaris. To get these new improved pasture species to grow and produce to their maximum my father was applying 125 kilograms per hectare of superphosphate every year on Winona, with some paddocks receiving over 4 tonnes per hectare during the next 35 years.

With a run of outstanding and wet seasons, Winona became very productive. Clover and grass grew over knee high and fed fat productive sheep. The sheep during this era cut enormous quantities of wool with stud ewes averaging eight kilograms each or double the amount of wool his sheep were producing previously. These high wool cuts coincided with the wool boom of the 1950s.

The Korean War started in 1950 and ended in 1953, and during this time the war generated an enormous demand for wool. American demand for wool created this short-lived and extreme increase in price when the United States bought large quantities to complete its strategic stockpiles. The need for wool created prosperity in the wool industry when the average greasy wool price reached 144.2 pence per pound, which is equivalent to around $37 per kilogram at today's prices. This is compared to recent prices of about $6 -$10 per kilogram, and fourteen times greater than the average, for the ten seasons ending in 1938-39 (10.39 pence per pound).

The period of high prices did not last and returns for wool quickly declined. In 1951-52 returns were half those received for the previous year. While small rises sometimes occurred over the next two decades, wool prices continued to drop until 1970-71, when the price fell to $0.60 per kilogram (equivalent to about $4 per kilogram in today's prices).

This period of high wool prices enabled Harry to buy more land, and in 1956 he purchased the adjacent 2000 acre (840 hectares) property Roxanna, on which he applied the same pasture improvement practices that were working so well on Winona. During this period he continued to add to the property by leasing 700 acres (291 hectares) on the western side of Winona called Old Hut. Harry was preparing for the future, and these additional areas of land would make the property large enough to divide for his three sons. My brother Ian would eventually own Roxanna, Barry would have Old Hut plus another block purchased in the 1960s, and I would inherit Winona. Due to Harry's excellent management and financial skills, his sons would own 2000 acres (840 hectares) each.

Even though this era was very productive and profitable, it was not without problems. The pastures that were dominated by sub clover had very high levels of phyto-oestrogen, which is a chemical that reduces female animal fertility and causes low birth rates. The effect of the oestrogen in the clover was very similar to putting the ewes on a birth control pill. Between 1950 and 1978 the numbers of lambs born declined to almost half of what were produced previously.

Merino sheep were never bred for grass as lush and green as the pastures now on Winona, and we were regularly trimming the sheep's feet to combat bacterial infection (foot abscess) caused by the animals continually having wet feet in the green pastures. The introduced pastures also increased problems with intestinal worms, creating the situation where we were treating (drenching) sheep every month.

The blowflies that had started to become an issue in the early 1900s for Nicholas and Granny had prospered through the decades. They were a significant problem for Harry in the

1950s because blowflies love wet wool to lay their eggs in, and on Winona, he had unknowingly created an issue with lush green pastures and sheep with very dense wool, which was a perfect environment. Harry mostly remedied this problem by selecting and breeding sheep that had white wool which was not affected by the high rainfall and consequently was less attractive to blowflies.

Through this era, the problems associated with sub clover and superphosphate were overlooked because the methods were continuing to be very profitable. An issue that had bothered my father for much of his farming life was the native red grass (Bothriochloa macra) invading his pastures. He regarded it as a problem because as it matured, it became inedible, and it was believed to choke out sub clover and reduce the quantity and quality of the pasture.

Harry solved this problem by ploughing paddocks every five years, sowing them to wheat and undersowing them with introduced, 'improved' pasture species. This process killed the red grass and enhanced the paddock with the newly planted pasture. The paddock was then annually fertilised with superphosphate.

I now realise that the red grass was covering the bare ground left by the introduced winter growing annual plants that did not grow during the summer. The clover wasn't choked out; it was shaded out by the red grass. The germinating clover seedlings, during autumn, require relatively bare ground to grow. If the paddocks were grazed differently, we would have clover growing over the winter period and red grass growing during the hot summer months.

Because Harry had killed the summer growing native grass by ploughing, then replaced it with winter-spring growing pasture, we were experiencing a period during the summer months with little pasture growth, even when it rained, because we had no summer species left to use the summer rainfall. Harry had seen a winter sheep feed deficit on Winona and, following the best scientific advice available, did an excellent job of fixing it, but he accidentally created a summer and autumn feed gap in its place. This annual summer drought was also caused by an abundance of sub-clover in late spring, which prevented many plants, including the native perennials, from germinating.

During the 1970s Harry started to put into place his planned family succession and his sons Barry, Ian and I would each start to manage their individual properties with the guidance of our father. Throughout this period we often worked together, sharing equipment and helping each other. The most significant event organised this way was the wheat harvest. In that era, we grew about three hundred acres (125 hectares) of wheat each, and all owned a harvester and truck, which was used to haul loads of grain to the local wheat delivery silo at Gulgong. It was a very efficient system. My two brothers and I operated a harvester each and Harry was the truck driver.

Harry was a great storyteller, which I am sure he inherited from his grandmother. He used to boast about how many truckloads of wheat he could deliver into the Gulgong silo in one day and claimed the record of fourteen loads over twelve hours. During that era, there was a lot of wheat grown around the district with many people delivering grain to the Gulgong silo. The other truck drivers could not understand how he could possibly drive a truck so fast to cover a thirty mile round trip in such a short time. Harry never told anyone that he was cheating and that we employed another man to help him. Our employee would fill the trucks with grain and start driving toward Gulgong to be met by Harry coming the other way with an empty truck, where they would switch vehicles and Harry would drive the newly filled truck to the delivery silo.

One day just as he pulled the truck to a stop at the delivery elevator he glanced down at the floor to see a six-foot black snake peacefully curled up at his feet. The very deadly black snake had most probably followed a mouse into the truck through a hole in the floor and then could not find his way out. On seeing the snake at his feet, Harry leapt from the truck and bolted across the paddock, creating a great source of amusement for the spectators in the other trucks. After recovering from shock and not intending to climb back into the snake-infested truck, Harry contacted me to come and get him, explaining there was a snake in the truck. The vehicle was left overnight with the door open to hopefully, allow the innocent snake to escape. On arrival next morning the other brave men in their delivery trucks had taken a wide berth around the snake contaminated truck. No one was brave enough to go near it. Dad suggested that I be the truck driver for the day, which I declined saying that he was the official truck driver. Gingerly poking his head in the door and thinking and hoping that the snake had moved on to annoy someone else, Harry climbed into the driver seat and resumed his wheat delivery. This event cured him of competing for record deliveries, but it started a new occupation: telling snake stories.

HOLES IN THE GREEN REVOLUTION

Even though this era was very productive and profitable, it was not without problems. The pastures that were dominated by sub clover had very high levels of phyto-oestrogen, which is a chemical that reduces female animal fertility and causes low birth rates. The effect of the oestrogen in the clover was very similar to putting the ewes on a birth control pill. Between 1950 and 1978 the numbers of lambs born declined to almost half of what were produced previously.

Merino sheep were never bred for grass as lush and green as the pastures now on Winona, and we were regularly trimming the sheep's feet to combat bacterial infections caused by the animals continually having wet feet in the green pastures. The introduced pastures also increased the rates of internal parasite infestations,, creating the situation where we were drenching sheep every month for worms

The blowflies that had started to become an issue in the early 1900s for Nicholas and Granny had thrived through the decades. They became a significant problem for Harry in the wet 1950s because blowflies love wet wool to lay their eggs, and on Winona he had unknowingly created an issue with lush green pastures and sheep with very dense wool, which was a perfect environment for blowflies. Over time, Harry remedied most of this problem by selecting and breeding sheep that had white, soft, wool, which was not affected by the high rainfall and consequently, was less attractive to blowflies.

Through this era, the problems associated with sub clover and superphosphate were overlooked because the methods were continuing to be very profitable. An issue that had bothered my father for much of his farming life was the summer-growing, native red grass (Bothriochloa macra) invading his pastures. He regarded it as a problem because as it matured, it became inedible, and it was believed to choke out sub clover and reduce the quantity and quality of the pasture.

Harry solved this problem by ploughing paddocks every five years, sowing them to wheat, and undersowing them with introduced, 'improved' pasture species. This process killed the red grass and enhanced the paddock with the newly planted pasture. The paddock was then annually fertilised with superphosphate.

I now realise that the red grass was covering the bare ground left by the introduced winter growing annual plants that did not grow during the summer. The clover wasn't choked out; it was shaded by the red grass. During autumn, the germinating clover seedlings require relatively bare ground to grow. If the paddocks were grazed differently, we would have clover growing over the winter period and red grass growing during the hot summer months.

Because Harry had killed the native grass, we were experiencing a period during the summer months with little pasture growth, even when it rained, because we had no summer species left to use the summer rainfall.

Harry had seen a winter sheep feed deficit on Winona and, following the best scientific advice available did an excellent job of fixing it, but he accidentally created a summer and autumn feed gap in its place. This annual summer drought was also caused by an abundance of sub-clover in late spring, which prevented many plants, including the native perennials, from germinating.

It became apparent in the early 1970s the high-input farming methods were not working as well as a decade previously. The wool boom of the 1950s was over, and farm incomes were significantly lower. Consequently, it was becoming difficult to justify the increasing costs to apply chemical inputs like fertiliser and pesticides that were necessary to prop up pastures and crops bred for the northern hemisphere that had better soil and more reliable rainfall. Secondly, but very significantly, the subsidised superphosphate, on which introduced plants like sub clover and ryegrass had become dependent, was no longer government financed. Superphosphate was almost ten times more expensive than thirty years previously. In 1968 the subsidised price of superphosphate was $16 per tonne, and ten years later in 1978 it cost over $52 per tonne, and in 1988 it was $160 per tonne.

As well as increasing costs it was also noted that the plants were failing to respond to the fertiliser and it became necessary to apply more to achieve the same response from the pastures. The decline in pasture growth was partly related to the soil becoming more acidic over time. This increasing soil acidity was created by the annual species of sub clover with the addition of superphosphate. Sub clover is a legume and is capable of producing significant amounts of nitrogen. As this nitrogen is leached from the root zone, it can increase soil acidity. This happens mainly because the pasture did not have any deep-rooted, long-lived perennial grass to trap and use the nitrogen before it moves from the root zone. In 1970 perennial grass was not the answer to fixing acid soil. Instead, an application of lime was the standard response and rates of two to three tonnes per acre were recommended by agricultural scientists to correct the problem.

So in the 1970s, as the wheels were falling off Winona, the best scientific advice of the day was making the problems worse, not better.

The problems continued to emerge, with significant saline outbreaks occurring over much of Winona. The dryland salinity that my father discovered as a fifteen-year-old in 1928 had increased from a small saline spring to cover over 100 acres (40 hectares) in 1975. The 100 acres of saline land was bare and eroded with deep gullies running through it. Because of the saline nature of the soil, it could no longer grow any grass to feed the sheep. There was a fear that the saline areas would continue to spread and eventually devastate much of Winona.

Years of ploughing the soil to grow wheat had left soil bare and destroyed the native grassland. The grassland that had controlled the hydrology of Winona for thousands of years was gone and replaced with introduced pasture with shallow root structures and an inability to grow during the hot summer months. These annual pastures could not possibly mimic native grasslands and their massive, fibrous root systems that absorbed moisture and regulated the water table.

Weeds were becoming a serious problem. As a teenager, I

remember the paddocks being yellow with capeweed and purple with Patterson's Curse. Annual weeds love the bare ground and weeds like saffron thistle, Patterson's Curse and silver grass, along with numerous other invasive species, were becoming abundant. With no known way of controlling the weeds they were accepted as normal, but the increasing weeds and decreasing pasture quality also started to impact on the sheep and wool production.

The agricultural advisers' common answer to this was to throw more money at the problem in the way of fertiliser and lime. This approach was of great concern to me. It was going to make the suppliers of the fertiliser wealthy and send us broke.

As the weeds increased and soil structure declined the pasture became less productive, and it became necessary to sow oats to feed the sheep through the winter months. The area to be planted with oats was prepared in a similar manner to growing wheat by being ploughed in December and cultivated three to four times before sowing the oat seed in March or April.

The summers also became increasingly difficult, not because it did not rain but because there were not many grass species that grew over the summer period. Years of ploughing had killed the summer growing native grass species, and with no summer sheep feed, it became necessary to sow millet as a forage crop in late spring to produce sheep feed during the summer months.

During the time my father farmed Winona he had owned many tractors. His old favourite was the 1930s Twin City, his least favourite a Lanz Bulldog from the late 1940s. In the 1960s the most popular tractor was an Australian made Chamberlain sixty horsepower tractor, and like most tractors sold before1980, it had no cabin.

One day as a teenager in October 1968 I was driving the Chamberlain tractor, sowing millet for summer forage. The tractor had no protection from the elements. Dust was flying everywhere, and I was forced to hold my breath when the wind blew from the wrong direction, to avoid choking on massive amounts of dust. As well as the dust to contend with I was swatting hundreds of flies all day as they buzzed around my face.

Anyone that has driven a tractor for days on end, ploughing or sowing paddocks, knows that there is plenty of time to think. Perhaps that is the only good thing about tractors! As I was driving in ever diminishing circles sowing millet seed, I started to think about the senselessness of what I was doing. There was something wrong if Winona could not produce enough pasture to feed our sheep through the summer without sowing millet or provide enough feed in the winter without sowing oats. Winona now lay bare and infertile, dependent on chemical inputs to produce pasture and crops. My great grandfather Nicholas had selected a property with beautiful grassland containing abundant species of grass, forbs and herbs. The combination of grassland and excellent soil fed Nicholas' sheep throughout the early years of pastoral colonisation. If I could restore the grassland, Winona would do that again.

During the 1970s, agricultural advisers said that if the use of superphosphate stopped, the introduced pastures of sub-clover and ryegrass would become unproductive. In the late 1970s, I began to doubt whether the agricultural methods of growing introduced pastures and propping those up with ever-increasing rates of fertiliser, could continue.

When Harry used superphosphate with his wheat crop in the 1930s, the response was dramatic and helped to produced exceptional yields. In the 1940s he discovered when the fertiliser was applied to clover the result was a significant increase in production from the clover, but over time a combination of superphosphate and clover created many problems on Winona. Harry started to observe problems in animal production like infertility in ewes and sheath rot in wethers. The high levels of soil phosphorus were causing unseen issues beneath the ground surface by creating an imbalance of soil microbes and increasing soil acidity. The prediction made to Harry in 1929 by his father that superphosphate would poison the ground was coming true. It was poisoning the ground in a very insidious manner, by killing soil fungi whose natural function was making phosphorus available to plants. With the fungi gone there was little phosphorus available except what was being applied as superphosphate. The plants became dependent on the annual dose of the fertiliser and required increasing amounts of superphosphate to maintain pasture and crop production.

The increasing problems with using superphosphate were many, but the most significant was one of economics. On Winona, spending over $50 000 (2015 figures) annually on fertiliser was hard to justify.

The decisions were made on Winona on a hot, windy day

in December 1979, by way of a major bushfire. It came out of the north-west and destroyed most of the buildings, three thousand sheep, all the pastures and sixty kilometres of fencing. It was the classic million-dollar fire that spiralled the family into massive debt.

❦ 2 ❦

FIRE

Before any humans inhabited the Australian continent over 60,000 years ago, the primary cause of fires would have been lightning. Over time Australia's original inhabitants learnt to harness these naturally occurring fires and they used it as a sophisticated tool to manage and modify the landscape. At pre-determined times of the year and with great skill they planned and carefully burned areas to encourage new growth of grassland plants, which provided productive feeding areas where browsing animals would graze the fresh shoots. This concentration of animals made them easier to hunt.

Some of the many benefits of managed fire are that it increased the productivity of certain varieties of food such as fungi and tubers and well as increasing the species diversity of grasslands from which seed was harvested to be ground and used to make rudimentary bread, among other things. Most of these fires were small-scale 'cool' fires, unlike the widespread, catastrophic hot fires caused by Europeans after they settled Australia.

The planned and precise fire management system developed and used over many thousands of years formed a 'mosaic' effect of differently burnt landscapes with varying ages. This allowed Indigenous people to create a series of diverse environments, expanding the variety of plants and animals available to them.

Since European settlement in Australia much of the traditional Indigenous land management methods have ceased to be used, and as a consequence severe, large-scale bushfires or wildfires, have become a significant problem, destroying homes, farms and towns. On such a vast continent these fires can cover huge tracts of land and burn for months before exhausting the supplies of fuel that sustains combustion. A severe bushfire can have a front of over thirty or forty kilometres and move faster than humans and animals can run, devastating everything in its path.

The native people have been gone from the area around Winona for over 100 years. Consequently, the region has not been managed with fire for a long period and the fire load or biomass of trees and understory in the bushland by the 1970s had built to very high and dangerous levels. Another massive change to the landscape has been the introduction of European grass and pasture species over Winona and much of the higher rainfall regions Australia.

The original Winona grassland consisted of a very diverse range of native plant species of which summer growing grasses dominated. The native summer grasses are usually green and actively growing during the summer months, unlike the introduced pasture species which tend to go dormant and are dry and brown during that period.

The local district around Winona had experienced an excellent season during most of 1979 with a huge growth of pasture until early October, when a not uncommon early hot spell hit, killing the introduced pasture plants and creating an enormous amount of tinder-dry highly combustible dead grass.

Harry had developed Winona into a picturesque property.

It was fenced with wooden posts and wire, into paddocks of around 100 acres each. The sub clover and ryegrass pasture, although dry in the summer months, was lush and green during spring and autumn. The Winona homestead that Harry had built for my mother Mari in 1939 was typical of Australian country homes, spacious with a large encircling veranda to shade it from the hot summer sun. One hundred meters north of the house stood the shearing shed. Like most of the buildings on Winona, it was clad in corrugated iron and constructed with timber cut from the property. The primary support structures were large round ironbark posts, and many of the internal sheep pens were made from round un-sawn pine railings which, over the years had been polished to a golden honey colour by the thousands of sheep that had been housed in the shed before they were shorn. One hundred meters to the west of the homestead was a rusty old shed, built in the 1940s to house farm machinery and another for the same purpose on the southern side of the house. About 500 meters to the west stood a shed, purpose-built to accommodate stud rams and ewes that were being prepared for show and sale.

It was nine a.m. on Sunday 16th December 1979, and the temperature was already over thirty degrees Celsius. Within two hours the temperature was approaching forty degrees and coupled with very low humidity and a fierce wind from the north-west there was a feeling of dread in the air. It was a perfect day for a fire.

At midday, as the temperature rose above 40 degrees Celsius a column of smoke was seen on the horizon.

I was turning thirty that year and not had a lot of experience fighting bushfires, but that was about to change with a quick, severe lesson in Australia's eucalypt fuelled fires. These are made far worse by the eucalyptus oil contained in the leaves of Australia's gum trees. The heat of the fire evaporates eucalyptus oil out of the leaves which become a volatile gas that burst into flames, often ahead of the main flames of the oncoming fire.

Harry had many years of experience with bushfires and was to be recognised, a few years later, for fifty years of dedicated service to the local Bushfire Brigade. He had seen the column of smoke from his house in the town of Gulgong which was twenty kilometres away and arrived in a rush expressing great concern and fear that this fire was to be a big one. Typical of my father's leadership qualities, those gathering to fight the fire were organised very quickly. I was to go with my Uncle and his seventeen-year-old son, Doug, on their truck to a neighbours' property. The vehicle was equipped with a water tank and a petrol driven firefighting water pump which, given the limited supply of water, was quite rudimentary by today's standards. Our job was to try to stop the fire as it came out of the scrubby hills and onto the dry grass areas on the neighbours' property. Harry would stay on Winona, muster the sheep and get them to safety.

We arrived at the neighbours' property as the fire was emerging from the thickly timbered country to see that four other local landowners were already at the fire with their small four-wheel drive trucks loaded with firefighting equipment and water tanks. One of the trucks was an ancient Bedford equipped with a fire pump of similar age. After the owner finally started the pump, which predated World War Two, he raced toward a small fire outbreak with a fire hose resembling an inferior irrigation system with water squirting everywhere except out of the end of the hose. For his safety, the owner of the old truck was finally encouraged to go with another, and better-equipped fire crew. As he climbed aboard, the fire exploded from the hills. It was obvious to us then that the fire was out of control and that it was not going to be stopped at the edge of the hills. It raced toward Gulgong faster than anyone could have imagined, and we looked on helplessly as the town was enveloped in smoke.

At that time we heard that there was a second, much larger inferno a few kilometres north- west of us was burning alongside the original fire. Everyone knew that all we could do was head towards own properties and protect the structures and animals from the fire as best we could. On arrival back at my Uncles property, I had no means of getting home and took the first vehicle I saw and headed to Winona.

At Winona, Harry was waiting with his small truck, equipped with pump and water tank. The fire was still in the hills three kilometres west of us, and it was obviously an enormous and scorching one that had spread over a vast area. My cousin and his son Trevor had arrived at 'Winona' earlier and had rescued some of the sheep. This quick thinking and excellent work saved many of them from being burnt to death.

Another neighbour, Bill McMaster and his 14-year-old son Stephen arrived with their old Austin fire truck to assist in protecting the Winona homestead, and shearing shed. Knowing that fire cannot travel across land already burnt, we decided to burn a fire-break one hundred metres west of the house and buildings to try to protect them. During our attempt to light this firebreak, the fire suddenly ignited the dry grass ahead of the fire and was coming at us at an astonishing speed about four hundred meters wide and twenty meters high.

Needing to escape the fire, Harry drove the truck with me on the back to a large area of bare ground near the Winona homestead. We arrived just as the fire hit. Trying to escape the intense heat, I jumped from the back of the truck and crawled under the back of the vehicle that I had previously commandeered and driven to Winona. The flames funnelled underneath the car, lighting my shirt and burning my head, arms and back. Needing to get away, and thinking that I was going to die because, as well as being alight, I was struggling to breathe the hot, oxygen-depleted air. The burning car exploded and propelled itself ten meters along the ground seconds after I was forced to find a safer place. Fortunately, I came across a truck and climbed into the passenger seat.   The difference in temperature in the cabin of the vehicle compared to the hot outside temperature was remarkable.

It is very difficult to put into words what it is like to be up close to a large fire.

What I remember most is the roaring sound of the fire coupled with the intense heat of the flames swirling around me and thinking I was going to suffocate. To be trapped in a fire is life and death. Fortunately, I made the right decisions at the right moments.

With the main part of the fire passing through Winona, Harry and I drove to inspect the shed in which over fifty rams and ewes were in preparation for various regional sales and shows around the state. The ram shed, built ten years previously, was specifically intended to house and prepare sheep for these shows and regional sales. It was built on the site of an old sheep camp with the thought that if sheep had wanted to be in that spot for the last hundred years, the conditions must be ideal there.

The shed was about five hundred metres from the homestead, and as I peered through the thick smoke, the shed looked to have escaped the fire. rams and ewes inside should be safe. But as we approached the building, it burst into flames. We had no choice but to look on hopelessly as the terrified, panicking sheep tried in vain to escape. Seeing the very best of Winona's stud rams and ewes dying in such a horrific manner was a very sombre experience.

Unable to do anything for the sheep, we drove back toward the house. Through the thick smoke, we could see that the shearing shed was alight and arrived in time to watch it burn and kill the five hundred stud ewes that Harry previously mustered and placed in the usually safe and cleared area of the sheep yards, adjacent to the shearing shed.

Unfortunately, no one had predicted the size and ferocity of the fire, and the shearing shed burned to the ground taking the sheep and yards with it.

We drove on a hundred meters through the thick, foul-smelling smoke to the homestead, which looked to have survived, until we saw that it was also burning. The fire quickly gained momentum, and soon the home, like the rest of Winona, was a smouldering ruin.

As we were looking at a lifetime of work being engulfed in flames, my cousin Trevor Seis appeared from the smoking ruins severely burned on the arms and back. Trevor had attempted to escape the fire by running into an open shed only to have the flames funnel into the shed, burning both him and the shed. Trevor had a knapsack with him and after dousing himself with water, ran back through the smoke and flames onto the blackened ground and escaped the fire.

At that moment, Bill McMaster emerged from the smoke, distraught that he could not find his son Stephen. Bill described how, when driving back towards the house after the fire had hit, he got lost in the smoke, could not see where he was driving, and ended up on the southern side of the house, one hundred meters from where he should have been.

The fire hit with such ferocity that the flames roared through the cab of the truck and he and his son Stephen were forced out of the truck. With his son beside him, Bill attempted to run back through the fire. Finally getting to safe ground, Bill realised Stephen wasn't with him.

Everything else was forgotten, and the five of us went on a frantic search for Stephen. Sadly, Harry found him dead against the back fence of the house; it appeared as though he was running toward the house for safety, but was unable to climb the four foot house fence. Between his senseless death and Winona being reduced to a smoking, depressing ruin, nothing else seemed to matter.

Harry and I got into his truck and started to drive to Gulgong through the very thick smoke and burned trees which had fallen across the road. While removing fallen trees from the road, I had realised for the first time I had been severely burnt. I had burned skin hanging from my underarms and back. My shirt was full of blackened holes, and my hair looked like a charred sock.

The last that I saw of the fire- front it was heading toward Gulgong at a very rapid pace, and we did not know whether the town had been reduced to rubble like Winona, or whether the people of Gulgong had escaped the fire.

My wife Kathy with our three children – Jason aged six, Rowena aged four, and Nicholas, just one month old – had attempted to get to Gulgong before the fire hit 'Winona' but were cut off by fire, could not get through, and returned to Winona. Fortunately, Harry instructed them to travel an alternate longer route to Gulgong, which circled the fire.

I did not know where they were, whether they had reached Gulgong or even if they were alive.

As we approached the township, we realised it had escaped unscathed. The wind had changed direction at the last minute and taken the fire away from the town. My family, the town and its inhabitants were safe.

Harry drove to his home in Gulgong, told my mother that we were fine, and drove me to Gulgong Hospital to be met by eight other people that had also been burned in the fire.

It was discovered that I had severe burns too many parts of my body and by this time I was suffering from shock. The days in the hospital were very painful, and I spent much of the time recollecting the events that happened before and during the fire.

In the period just before the fire hit Winona, my 6-year-old son, Jason let all the dogs off their chains, thinking they would have a better chance of survival.

A six-month-old kelpie male pup called Joe, who was showing great potential as a working dog, lived around the house with the orphaned lamb. He survived by getting on the verandah of the house with the lamb and both emerged out of the smoke as the house was burning. Joe went on to be the leading sire of the 'Winona Kelpie Stud,' breeding many hundreds of pups and was very well known around the state, having worked in sheepdog trials as well as countless demonstrations at field days and shows.

The orphaned lamb grew into an excellent ram and became an influential sire for Winona, helping to rebuild the genetics of the Winona merino stud.

Of the dogs that Jason set free, Cher was a 4-year-old stud bitch, which I had recently purchased. She survived by jumping into the water of a nearby dam and like Joe, emerged through the smoke after the fire had passed. She was pregnant at the time. Two days after the fire on the 18th December she had eight pups. One, named 'Ashes', went on to be an excellent breeding bitch for the "Winona" Kelpie

Stud. Maddie, a black & tan bitch, was never found. Trixie, a red and tan bitch, was last seen sheltering from the fire behind the tractor, and I assumed that she, like Maddie had been killed. The tractor, parked on bare ground between the house and shed, was still connected to the harvester that, the previous day, had finished harvesting the last of the 1979 wheat crop.

Trixie was an excellent sheepdog, and would work ewes with their lambs in a soft, quiet manner, never hurrying them. She was equally as good in the rugged timbered country on the south of Winona and would gently bring large mobs out of difficult to muster areas, in her usual no-fuss manner.

During the third day that I was in the hospital, a nurse came to me to ask if I owned an old red and tan kelpie bitch, reporting that one was lying on my burned clothes that had been placed in the garbage bins at the back of the hospital. After telling the nurses that I have an old dog that fitted the description, but she had died in the fire, they chased her away. The next day the old dog had mysteriously returned, removed the clothes from the rubbish bin and was again, lying on them. The nursing staff thought this very unusual, so instead of chasing her away again, they took me to see the dog.

Trixie was definitely not dead; she was lying on my burned clothes and wouldn't leave. She was very loyal and would always be by my side no matter what I was doing, but this was taking loyalty to another level. Trixie had never been to the hospital or even Gulgong before, having been born and spent all of her life on the farm. To this day, it is not known how she found me at the hospital which was over 20 kilometres from her home. I was worried about Trixie wandering off and getting lost, or someone stealing her, so Harry came and picked her up and took her back to Winona. Trixie lived to old age doing what she loved, mustering sheep, and she also produced many pups that continue her legacy in the Winona dogs today.

It was almost Christmas, and the care and generosity of the people of Gulgong and district were remarkable. Children's Christmas gifts and anonymous cash donations appeared on the steps of my parent's Gulgong house. The entire Gulgong community showed immense grief and genuine concern.

While in the hospital I was unaware of what was happening at home on 'Winona'.

Many local people and neighbours arrived to help euthanize and bury burned, suffering sheep. I was fortunate to miss out on this terrible job of shooting hundreds of severely burned animals.

Many town people, farming families and neighbours arrived with trucks, tractors, shovels chainsaws and bare hands to Winona to clean up the mess of tangled burned roofing iron, burned water tanks and the stinking dusty ash from remains of the house, sheds and fences. A far worse and very depressing task was to bury the dead and by now, rotting, dead, blackened sheep.

This was a sad time for my father, who had spent his life breeding the sheep which he cared greatly for. Many of the dead ones were piled on top of each other against fences where they had tried to in vain to escape the fire. These sheep were buried where they lay, but the many hundreds of sheep that were scattered over the property could not be buried or picked up; Winona was dotted with burned decaying carcasses for many months. These took a long time to decompose because the fire was so hot and on such a large scale that the flies and insects that would normally help in the decomposing process had also been killed.

The losses on Winona were massive.

Three thousand sheep were killed. The homestead, shearing shed, machinery shed, truck, car and most of

Winona's 50 kilometres of fencing were all gone. But this is insignificant when compared to the loss of Stephen McMaster's life.

However, some things did survive. One building was left standing after the fire. An old machinery shed, which was burning when my brother Barry arrived a few hours after the fire had passed and he extinguished the burning posts and rafters; the charred posts are still in the old shed today.

The fire did not only destroy Winona. It covered a large portion of the district, burning thousands of acres, as well as homes, sheds, cars, hundreds of kilometres of fencing and livestock. The livestock killed in the disaster numbered over sixteen thousand sheep as well as countless cattle and horses.

In the 1970s the ewes on Winona gave birth to their lambs in autumn, so the rams were with the ewes at the time of the fire.

In the hurry to save sheep, fifty-two ewes and their ram Walter, were placed in a small set of yards adjacent to the ram shed. One gate had a faulty catch that I had intended to fix for some time. As the fire engulfed the shed, the ewes panicked and rushed the gate, which broke the catch and flung the gate open. The ewes and Walter escaped to freedom and safety.

When Harry was mustering sheep and putting them in safer places, he could not locate one mob of fifty stud ewes with their ram Charles. Charles was the great- great grandson of Bill, the original Winona sire who won Champion Ram at the Sydney sheep show in the early 1950s. Like his famous ancestor, Charles had won numerous awards around the state earlier in 1979, and I assumed that Charles and his ewes had died in the fire like most of the sheep on Winona.

Four days after the fire, while I was still in the hospital, Harry was cleaning up the remains of the smoking black ruins of the shearing shed and sheep yards. Looking up, he saw a small mob of sheep walking toward him, stirring the thick black dusty soot as they went. Charles, blackened by the smoke, arrived at the yards leading his fifty equally soot covered ewes. Charles was fed oats and chaff while being exhibited at the local shows and had returned looking for more oats and chaff and because all of the grass on 'Winona' had been burned.

Harry was so pleased to see them he gave them oats from one of the surviving grain silos and placed them in a small paddock so he could better look after the precious ram, ewes and Charles's unborn lambs they were carrying.

The two rams Charles and Walter with their ewes and unborn lambs were to be the foundation of the resurrected Winona Merino Stud that continues today.

One thousand sheep amazingly survived the fire. Sheep have a survival instinct of circling in a tight mob when confronted with danger. This usually happens when being attacked by predators but in this situation the predator was fire. The sheep on Winona were run in mobs of three hundred, and as the fire hit, they instinctively milled into a tight group. The sheep on the outside of the mob were killed, but the sheep in the centre were protected by the ones on the edge. Most of the sheep that lived through the ordeal were burned on the face and legs, but their wool protected the rest of their body. Many of the survivors had their ears burned off, and the ones with ears had their plastic ear tags, melted into them.

Ewes are usually sold as they reach middle age of five years old. Harry and I did not have the heart to sell the ewes as they got older after surviving such an ordeal. We thought they had earned the right to live their whole life on Winona, so they were kept on Winona until they died of old age Many of these ewes lived and reared lambs until the grand old age of twelve and thirteen years old.

We used to run about one hundred Red Poll cows on Winona as another enterprise. The mob of cows and calves were in an area of Winona where the fire was not as fierce. The cattle panicked and ran back through the fire, and all survived. Rather than try to feed the cattle they were sold and the money used to help rebuild Winona.

Winona, the homestead, shearing shed, buildings, fencing and sheep were Harry's life's work, and he could never look at the place in the same way again. 'His Winona had been destroyed forever'. However, my father was a very strong person, and together we set about rebuilding.

COLIN SEIS

REBUILDING WINONA.

With the Winona homestead destroyed, having
somewhere to live was a priority. The Rouse family is one of
the original squatter families in the district, and Richard
Rouse had a cottage on his property 'Birkalla' just ten
kilometres away from Winona. Richard very kindly gave us
the cottage rent free while the new homestead was being built
during 1980. During the building of the new Winona house, I
learned a lot of new things, becoming a 'brickie's labourer, an
electrician's apprentice, a builder's assistant, and a cabinet
maker. I excelled in none of these trades, but the job was
completed by Christmas that year, with excellent help from
my brothers in- law who all had building trades.

While I was helping to build the house, Harry and my
brother Barry were designing and building the shearing shed.
They searched the country for the best designs and completed
the four stand shed around the same time that I finished
building the house.

In the meantime, people from all over the district and
surrounding towns arrived to repair many of the burned

fences, and by 1982 the buildings and many of the fences were replaced.

I cannot fully express my appreciation for the work that they did.

The rebuilding of Winona was a daunting task, made worse by having no money and massive debt. The whole farm had been destroyed, and everything had to be replaced. Even the pasture had been killed in areas where the fire was so intense that it baked the ground. In reality, it has taken my whole working life, until now, to complete the rebuilding.

1980 was a tough year for many reasons. As well as rebuilding the house, shed, and fences, it did not rain for many months, which made the soot-laden dust, which got in eyes, nose, and mouth, much worse.

On the positive side, many of the surviving one thousand sheep were placed on properties around the district. This took the pressure off Winona and allowed us more time to re-build fences and infrastructure and gave the pasture on Winona the opportunity to recover.

How we survived financially, I am still not sure. We had a considerable debt after rebuilding and far less income because the low sheep numbers, and the fire- affected sheep, did not produce as much wool as in previous years. Also, we were selling very few surplus sheep because all the ewes were kept on 'Winona' to produce lambs.

New directions

Australia is a tired old country and was quietly happy in her old age until Europeans arrived in 1788. During the next 200 years, Europeans enforced modern agriculture upon her by ploughing her already fragile soil, forcing upon her high inputs of artificial fertiliser and pesticides as well as introducing plants that were never intended to grow in her soil. The new settlers had no understanding of Australia's unique ecosystems that had been so carefully and wisely managed for many thousands of years by the country's original custodians. It should be no surprise that she eventually objected to the abuse and responded in the form of extreme salinity, acid soils, dying rivers, and dying plants?

It is inconceivable to imagine a culture continuing and thriving in an arid, hot and ancient continent for 2000 human generations, but Australia's Indigenous people had successfully learned to coexist with this great southern land for over 50,000 years

The Australian Indigenous people had protected and nurtured their rivers, grasslands and ecosystems for over five millenniums. They learned to live harmoniously with the land, but the agricultural methods that I had adopted were doing the opposite; destroying rivers, grasslands and ecosystems. This made me realise that I should look at how they lived so successfully and somehow incorporate their management, or at least their philosophy, into Winona's management.

A lot more would be added to my basic knowledge when I met local a Indigenous elder, David Maynard, and learned to look at how nature works. David is a very kind and patient man who spoke with immense passion about his people's spiritual connection to the land. He explained in far more detail than could ever be learned from a book about how his people managed the land. With David's teaching, I became more aware of the interconnectedness of nature, how ecosystems worked, and how everything is complimentary when it is managed as nature designed it.

David also added to my interest in native grass species, the seed of many being an important food source for Indigenous populations. If Indigenous people ate native grass seed for many thousands of years why couldn't it be used as a food source for people of the world?

European farming methods overlaid with a philosophy of

caring for Winona's ecosystem would be a critical part of Winona's future management and the interconnectedness of everything would be the answer in my quest to reduce cost and increase production.

Life was difficult on Winona during the 1980s. The fire had cost us a massive amount of money, and our income was severely depleted because of low sheep numbers. Winona's dry-land salinity problems were getting worse, and the fertiliser and clover induced acid soil was also limiting production. I was trying to plan how we could survive financially and had fleeting thoughts of growing wheat on all of Winona for a few years. This could have generated more income but would have involved ploughing all of 'Winona's' soil, killing the grass and destroying the very last remnants of Winona's grassland plants. The long-term consequences of that were not acceptable; I had to find another way. I would reduce the money that was being spent on Winona. In other words, I would develop a very low input, low-cost method, of running the property .

One of my most significant costs was fertiliser. Harry had been applying 125 kilogrammes per hectare of superphosphate to the pastures annually since the early 1950s. This amount of fertiliser had made Winona very productive, but was now too expensive to apply. I realised I could no longer afford the superphosphate that best science and best advice insisted we continue to use. During the 1970s and 1980s using large amounts of fertiliser was a sign of a good farmer, and farmers used to boast about how much superphosphate they applied. Bad farmers were the ones that used no fertiliser or had native grass pastures, not the new "improved" introduced pastures, that grew very well while propped up with ever-increasing amounts of fertiliser.

I could no longer afford the superphosphate and pasture seed that was costing over a quarter of my annual income. The advice given to people with introduced pastures is that fertiliser needs to be applied annually to make the grass more productive. Knowing that if fertiliser were no longer used, and I restored the native grassland, I would be strongly criticised, so I told no-one about my plans or what I was doing until many years later.

I approached this problem another way. If the pastures on Winona were dependent on an annual "fix", to grow, maybe we would be better without them and have plants that were not addicted to superphosphate and would grow well without it. In other words, over the years on Winona, we were growing plants that wanted to die and killing plants that wanted to live.

It was a big gamble, but I had no other option. I thought that if superphosphate were no longer used, native grass species that were not dependent on high levels of phosphorus would return.

The agronomy experts were correct when saying production would fall if the application of pasture fertiliser were stopped. After deciding not to apply the annual dose of superphosphate, the next 7-8 years production from the introduced pastures declined dramatically and eventually most of the perennial ryegrass, and much of the clover died. As the fertiliser dependent plant species died, native grass species started to appear.

The first grass to return was native red grass. *(bothriochloa macra)*. It is a summer growing perennial species which my father regarded as poor quality sheep feed. He battled for years trying to eradicate red grass and when it started to appear in paddocks was an indication that it was time to plough the paddock and re-sow it with clover and ryegrass. I now understand that the red grass was invading and colonising the annual pasture and if left would have evolved into grassland with a mix of summer and winter plant species.

What was a significant problem for my father was rapidly

becoming Winona's saviour. Red grass can be an inferior quality grass species if grazed inappropriately, but as soil health improves with better, more appropriate management, the sheep-feed quality also improves. Red grass is an early colonising grassland species, which prepares the soil and ground cover conditions for other, better quality perennial species.

I would use red grass to restore Winona's native grassland.

Weeds

Weeds are a symptom of the land management methods.

For many years the summers on Winona were dry and challenging because not many grass species grew during this period since the last of the better quality grassland species had been removed many years previously by ploughing to grow wheat crops. The loss of these warm-season grasses created a second problem; the property had bare ground in the autumn months when temperature conditions are ideal for the germination of annual weeds. The ground cover and soil on Winona had been declining for many years and with bare soil came a lot of annual weeds like purple flowered Patterson's Curse and yellow capeweed. These plants germinated on autumn rain, and being annual colonising species; they love bare soil. Annual weeds worry many people because they can limit production and advisers tell them that they will dominate pastures and be tough to eradicate. The advice at the time was to control them by ploughing or use herbicide to kill them. This recommendation is still given today.

I did not follow the advice to kill them but let them do what 'Mother Nature' designed them to do; cover bare ground. I started to create and maintain ground cover by using the weeds to grow litter, cover the soil, and improve soil structure with their aggressive root systems. By letting weeds do what they are designed to do they helped in the restoration of Winona and paved the way for more native perennial grass species to return.

Using weeds to fix soil and start a grassland restoration process was contrary to any agronomic advice and was sure to attract criticism. I am certain that anyone who knew what I was doing, would think I was mad.

Toward the end of the 1980s, I started to see Winona change. Weeds like 'capeweed' and 'Patterson's Curse' were disappearing as the soil improved and good quality native grass species like wallaby grass, *(danthonia sp.)* Warrego (*paspalidium sp.*) and native forbs started to replace the weeds. These species had not been on Winona for fifty to sixty years, and it made me realise that it may be possible to restore the property to the grassland that my great grandparents had over one hundred and forty years previously.

Saline Areas

Salt has naturally accumulated in Australia's soil over many thousands of years from weathered parent rocks, ocean salt carried inland by the wind, and evaporation of inland seas. This salt is usually not a problem unless groundwater and rising water tables mobilise it.

Prior to British settlement in 1788, groundwater levels were kept stable by grasslands and their associated trees and shrubs. Inappropriate grazing practices and ploughing soil to grow crops removed grassland species that were often replaced with shallow-rooted pasture plants which were unable to intercept and absorb stored and rising groundwater. This created an imbalance in the hydrological cycle and resulted in dryland salinity.

Over time, in some areas of Australia, this process has caused the topsoil to become irreversibly saline, and no longer suitable for agriculture. In Australia an estimated 2.5million hectares of land had become salinised since the introduction of European farming methods and, around 5.7million hectares of land is classed as having 'high potential' for salinisation,

Saline soil can decrease the ability of plants to absorb water through their roots via osmosis and, cause leaf burn, resulting in reduced growth, and plant death.

The saline areas that Harry had discovered as a sixteen-year-old in 1928 continued to grow larger over the years of ploughing, growing wheat crops and annual, introduced pasture. By the late 1980s, one hundred acres or five percent of the total property was severely affected by salt and the potential for half of Winona to become affected was a real possibility, if the farming methods did not change.

In the late 1980s, I decided to try to do something about the saline areas and contacted the local government soil conservation officer, who made a property visit and suggested many positive changes. One of the more unusual suggestions was to form a Landcare group. Landcare is a Government supported, Australia wide, grassroots movement started in 1986 that encourages individuals and groups to protect, restore and sustainably manage Australia's natural environment, and improve agricultural productivity, through sustainable land management.

The Landcare movement had only just begun, and I knew nothing about it. However, I started the 'Barneys Reef Salinity Landcare Group' to secure some funding for salinity trials on Winona.

To form a Landcare group required a president, secretary and treasurer. At that time there was no one else interested, so I became the president, secretary, treasurer and only member of 'Barneys Reef Landcare Group'. I do not think the bureaucrats would allow that to happen today. However, I generated interest in the project and soon had my brother Barry, cousin Doug and neighbour Daryl Cluff, on board. Daryl Cluff was to become an important addition to the work at Winona for other reasons a few years later. This small band expanded over the years and did some amazing things like invent and build one of Australia's first native grass seed harvesters, plant tens of thousands of trees, fence remnant tree and grassland areas and learn how to harvest, and sow native grass seed.

Forming the Landcare group was a catalyst to fix the salinity problem, and Winona became one of the major experimental dry land salinity sites in NSW, being driven by Alan Nicholson who went on the become one of the leading salinity experts in Australia.

The sites were contoured and sown with salt tolerant grass species which worked well, but I realised that the landscape had to be repaired if I was to fix the problem permanently.

Daryl Cluff and I recognised that native grass or more accurately, native grassland, was the answer. The saline areas were just a symptom of a broken ecosystem which expressed itself with, poor hydrology or distribution and circulation of water in the soil. Native grassland with its very diverse range of grass and forbs had managed the groundwater for millennia, and if the grassland was restored, it could do it again.

To fix the salinity problem I needed to restore grassland over the area where water was entering the landscape, which was almost all of Winona, but no one knew whether it was possible to establish native grass over the entire property.

Our interest in native grass expanded so Daryl Cluff and I thought we would learn more about different species from an expert, but there was only one in all of Australia:, Professor Wal Whaley at the University of Armidale.

Much of the knowledge about native grass had been lost

because years of research into introduced pasture species that started in the 1920s had been at the expense of lost knowledge in Australian native grass species. We then realised if anything were to be done with reinstating the knowledge of native grass, we would have to do it ourselves.

In 1997 Daryl Cluff, with the help of Professor Whaley, organised a meeting which attracted a surprising number of other people interested in native grass. This resulted in the formation of the 'Stipa Native Grass Association' which has now grown to be a very influential Australia wide organisation dedicated to the practical application of native grass species and restoring and managing native grasslands.

❧ 3 ❧

FARMING HISTORY

My great-grandfather, grandfather and father had all been successful farmers and had adopted 'best practice' farming methods during their era. They had managed their sheep and grown crops so successfully that the original forty-acre farm that Nicholas bought in 1868 had now been expanded by Nicholas, then Joseph and Harry. Today Nicholas' descendants own almost twelve thousand acres in the immediate area around the original farm that Nicholas selected.

Why then, near the end of the 20th century, one hundred and forty years after Nicholas started farming, was Winona's soil hard, compacted, lifeless, and dysfunctional? Why did Winona have so many unproductive weeds? Where had the grassland gone? Why was it necessary to apply large quantities of chemical fertiliser and use life destroying pesticides?

I was now custodian of Winona, and if the property was to continue into the future, it was vital to uncover what went wrong and how I could fix it. My quest to restore the family farm would need to answer these questions.

Perhaps the answer lay at the very beginning of

agriculture, in Mesopotamia ten thousand years ago. Did the original creators of agriculture get it wrong? Was the adoption of their methods by Western agriculture the wrong model to follow?

Around 12,000 years ago, as the last ice age was retreating, around Western Asia, in what is commonly called the Fertile Crescent, the climatic conditions were arid and cold. This extreme weather killed much of the wildlife the early hunter-gatherers depended on, forcing the people to eat seeds of grass which they eventually learned to grow and then harvest later in the season. Agriculture was born.

The Fertile Crescent is a crescent-shaped region containing the fertile land of otherwise arid and semi-arid Western Asia, and the Nile Valley. It also includes ancient Mesopotamia, the land in and around the Tigris and Euphrates rivers. The area was the centre of domestication of three cereal plants (einkorn wheat, emmer wheat and barley) and four legumes (lentil, pea, bitter vetch and chickpea). These plants now make up a substantial percentage of the world's food supply.

For over 10,000 years the Sumerian people of Mesopotamia, developed and practised agriculture on the alluvial plains of the Tigress and Euphrates Rivers. (Mesopotamia includes most of modern-day Iraq, and parts of Syria, Iran, and Turkey). The very early methods used to plant crops around the Fertile Crescent are not known, but it is assumed the method used to prepare the soil for planting would have originally been prehistoric digging sticks. Over time these digging sticks were modified and eventually fitted with handles for pulling and pushing. Domestication of oxen in Mesopotamia, about 8000 years ago provided the Sumerians with the draft power necessary to develop an animal-drawn scratch plough called an Ard. The Ard was dragged through the topsoil to cut a shallow furrow suitable for most cereal crops. A method of sowing seeds invented by the Mesopotamians, about 3500 years ago, was a significant technological achievement. It revolutionised agriculture by carrying out the tasks of seeding and ploughing simultaneously, by dropping seed down a tube into the furrow that the plough created.

The arid climate of Mesopotamia encouraged the development of irrigation and produced grain in quantities greater than the people's current needs, freeing them to do other things instead of growing food. The freedom from growing food gave rise to what we call civilisation, and this freedom was most likely instrumental in the invention of the wheel which was utilised for everyday use around 5500 years ago. They have also been credited with inventing sails, which were used to harness the wind, to move small boats. The sail was important in helping to stimulate the growth and development of trade along the Tigris and Euphrates rivers. The Mesopotamians also invented some of the earliest forms of writing which contributed to advance the growth and development of complex societies in Mesopotamia and later in other areas of the world.

These agricultural methods worked well for hundreds of years until excessive ploughing and overgrazing of grasslands in the headwaters and catchment of the Tigress and Euphrates Rivers created significant soil erosion of these areas. The water, heavily laden with silt and mud, spilt over the floodplains of the two rivers depositing of as much as four meters of sediment over the area including ancient Babylonia, which was the capital of most of the civilised world 4,000 years ago. As the muddy river water slowed down and dumped silt, it choked the irrigation canals with mud, making it necessary to de-silt the canals year after year to supply life-giving water to farmlands and cities of the plain. As populations grew, canals were extended further and further from the rivers, until the vast system of canals required a considerable amount of hand labour to keep them clean of silt. The mud clearing became an endless imposition on the people and may have been instrumental in the decline of Babylon, which had stood for thousands of years.

The silt-laden water continued its journey down the rivers and into the Persian Gulf, where the deposited mud has created thirty meters of land annually since Sumerian times. The ancient city of Ur, birthplace of Biblical figure Abraham, was once a thriving seaport but now its ruins lie almost 240 kilometres inland. The continual dumping of silt and mud around the mouth of the Euphrates eventually changed the course of the river and ultimately contributed to its final decline.

The problems did not stop with silt and mud; the agricultural methods were creating another, more insidious problem for Mesopotamia. The alluvial soils of Southern Mesopotamia are rich in salts carried down from the mountains by the Tigris and the Euphrates rivers. These salts tend to accumulate in the water table and can are toward the surface either through capillary action or through rising of the water table. The same process that allowed farming in this region also eventually led to its downfall by making it impossible to farm. Irrigation has a downside: if irrigation water is allowed to sit on the fields and evaporate, it leaves behind mineral salts which become toxic to plants. In Mesopotamia, irrigation was essential for crop production, and as the water evaporated, it left its dissolved mineral salts behind and also drew salts upward from lower levels of the soil.

Wheat had been grown in Mesopotamia for thousands of years, but as the soil became saline, the yields declined to a point where more salt-resistant barley replaced wheat. Eventually the land became excessively saline even for the salt-resistant barley, and eventually becoming so salty it could not sustain the growth of any crops at all. Within a few thousand years agricultural production in Mesopotamia was reduced to a tiny fraction of what it had been. Many fields were abandoned as useless for agriculture.

It has been estimated that it was possible in ancient times to irrigate thirteen million acres of the alluvial soil of Mesopotamia; the population of Mesopotamia at its peak was probably between seventeen and twenty-five million people. The current population of all Iraq is estimated to be about four million including nomads. Of this total less than four million live on the alluvial plain.

The agricultural methods developed in Mesopotamia were adopted by the Egyptians and later by the Romans. Around the Mediterranean region, Romans advanced agriculture to another level with the development of a better, more efficient, plough with iron shares which was pulled by oxen. The Romans also discovered that if animal manure was added to the fields and then the fields ploughed twice at right angles to each other, they would achieve better yields. Later the development of a heavier wheeled plough, initially drawn by oxen and then by horses, made possible the northward spread of agriculture into Europe.

Modern agriculture is based on these methods developed in Mesopotamia over ten millennia ago, then later adopted and modified by Romans and Europeans. The problem with establishing modern agriculture on the Mesopotamian model is that it failed many thousands of years ago and modern agriculture is also failing and causing severe land degradation and dessertifications around the world. Why has this form of agriculture and its adoption around the world failed? Did we get agricultural principles and practices wrong from day one? Did the Sumerians go down the wrong track agriculturally? Maybe our adoption of their techniques was not the best agriculture practice to implement.

There are examples of sustainable, ecologically based agriculture being adopted in other countries around the world that have been practised for at least as long as the Sumerians

The transition from hunter-gatherer to agricultural societies occurred in many countries around the world almost simultaneously. In China, rice and millet were domesticated around 10,000 years ago while in New Guinea, early Papuan communities are thought to have begun practising agriculture around 9,000 years ago with the cultivation of sugarcane and root crops and the domestication of pigs.

Along the Indus valley in the present-day region of Pakistan and India, there is evidence of wheat and legume crops and domestication of sheep and goats over 8 000 years ago. The Indian elephant was also domesticated soon after this time.

Mesoamerica, which means "middle America", is a region and cultural area in the Americas, which extended north and south from its cultural centre in southern Mexico. For many thousands of years, the area has been inhabited by numerous groups of people including the Olmec, Zapotec, Teotihuacan, Mixtec, Totonac, Maya and Aztec. At the time of the arrival of the Spaniards in 1519, Mesoamerica was populated by an estimated 25 million people who were practising a very advanced form of agriculture. Many types of crops were developed which included hundreds of varieties of squash, beans, cocoa and corn. Maize was bred from a wild annual grass called teosinte which was transformed through human selection into the ancestor of modern corn, more than 6,000 years ago. It gradually spread across North America and was a significant crop of Native Americans at the time of European exploration.

Further south, in what is now the Andes region of South America, complex societies, were in existence by around 3000 BC. The agricultural communities of the Andean civilisations developed the potato, as well as varieties of beans, and domesticated llamas, alpacas, and guinea pigs many thousands of years ago.

Indigenous Australians are the oldest continuous culture on the planet. They are thought to be descendants of the first people to leave Africa between 64,000 and 75,000 years ago and are believed to have arrived in Australia over 60,000 years ago.

From the early days of European settlement, Indigenous Australians have been characterised as being nomadic hunter-gatherers who did not develop agricultural practices or other forms of food production. However, more recent explanations of Indigenous life have lead to discoveries that they had been developing a type of agriculture and cultivation which was a feature of Indigenous land use. Archaeological research in south-west Victoria and Northern New South Wales has shown sophisticated eel farming and fish trapping systems that had been developed over a period of many thousands of years. Early forms of agriculture were also being practised, with plants like yams being sown and cultivated. Seed from native grassland species were harvested on a large scale with grain stored for later use. It is now known that people in many regions were living in permanent settlements like towns, with between 200 to 500 residents in dwellings that housed 10 or more people.

There is evidence to suggest that agriculture is possibly older in Africa than Mesopotamia, with examples of animal domestication 15,000 years ago and crop cultivation 18,000 years ago in the Great Rift Valley of Ethiopia which is often regarded as the birthplace of *Homo Sapiens*.

Rising high above East Africa's Rift Valley are the luxuriant hills of the Gamo Highland people. The Gamo people have been farming in the area for at least as long as the Sumerians of Mesopotamia, and it is believed the techniques used today in the Gamo Highlands were developed over 10,000 years ago. How did the Gamoens and many other cultures develop an agriculture system that has continued for millennia, while the Sumerian methods in Mesopotamia failed?

While much of Africa has suffered famines and food shortages, the Gamo region has been sheltered from much of these problems due to the unique traditional agricultural systems that account for the ecology of the area, which interweaves livestock production with a diverse number of cereal crops, vegetable crops and forestry. The Gamo system of management, conservation, and preservation of soil, water, pasture and forest are all interconnected, and they understand that all aspects of nature are required to be in balance. They only take what is needed from the land and know what the earth needs to replenish itself. Because they have managed their farms as ecosystems for millennia, the whole area now has an enormous diversity of plant species for food production and ecosystem balance. The agricultural system integrates a vast genetic diversity of crop species, ranging from one hundred enset (false banana), sixty barley and twelve wheat varieties, as well as numerous varieties of taro, yams and potato.

A collection of complex and well-enforced traditional laws define how their land is managed. These laws are enforced by a Council of Elders, in the same manner as their ancestors have done for many thousands of years. The Elders administer the rotation of grazing lands, when and where to plant crops, plan ceremonies, resolve disputes and enforce the strict rules that protect sacred places throughout the Gamo Highlands.

These laws stem from the belief that everything is connected and bound in a delicate balance, and this forms a natural management system that dictates everything from interpersonal relationships to the conservation and preservation of pasture, forest, soil, and water. Such is their understanding of their interconnected ecosystem; if there is a problem then the whole system is understood to be at risk.

The Gamoens, or more specifically the elders that enforce land management methods, understand the interconnectedness of nature. They are aware that the forest with its diverse range of trees and plants protect and filter water of silt and impurities. The grassland is used for grazing animals and the manure from the animals used as fertiliser for crops. They are aware of the importance of having the correct balance and numbers of animals to supply enough nutrients for crops but not have too many animals as to degrade the grassland.

It could be said that the Gamo people and their agricultural methods have survived because of a small population. In fact the Gamo Highlands are one of the most densely populated parts of rural Africa and is currently home to one million people. A people whose ecological farming methods and culture have remained intact in spite of modern agricultural practices from the outside world and pressure to change. That is until now.

The Gamoans and their spiritual connection to the land, is intertwined with the ecology of the land, but their methods of agriculture are under extreme external threat from Christian religious groups and multinational companies. With the fanaticism of 19th-century missionaries, the religious groups are challenging the Gamo people's spiritual connection to the land, eroding the traditional social structures that have bound the people of the Gamo to each other and the environment, for millennia. Multinational companies, under the disguise of Green Revolution in Africa (AGRA), are forcing Western chemical agriculture upon them. By giving the farmers loans, the farmers are encouraged by AGRA to use external inputs, such as genetically modified seeds, chemical pesticides and fertilisers. The religious groups and AGRA are most likely well-intentioned, but an agricultural system that has worked so well for 10,000 years should be looked upon in awe, not looked down upon with Western arrogance.

This type of arrogance occurred against many native people and their cultures as Europeans expanded into the world many hundreds of years ago and enforced their form of agriculture and religion onto people that had flourished for many thousands of years. The kind of agriculture imposed on many countries and cultures destroyed the delicate ecological balance that most of these ancient societies had in place, and destroyed the grasslands, farming areas and the people themselves.

Modern Agriculture with its flawed sense of separation from, and superiority over nature, has reduced our most important food crops to just a few species, which has potentially severe consequences for world food security and world ecosystems. The Gamo people have learned to conserve plant genetic species while practising highly productive farming methods and have hundreds of food species, which challenges the assumption that intensive agriculture decreases biodiversity.

Many of the world's native people and cultures are embedded in an ecosystem that is intensively managed and yet, unlike our industrialised agriculture, includes an astonishing amount of diversity, stability and resilience. Over thousands of years, they have developed a way of being in the world that has ensured their long-term existence. The management of their whole ecosystem; from water tables, soil nutrient cycles and social infrastructure, stems from a view of the world as sacred, alive and entirely interconnected.

There is much to learn from many of the world's native people and cultures. Western agriculture with its superiority over nature was flawed from the beginning and is failing. Maybe we have had it wrong for 10,000 years. A serious problem with Mesopotamian agriculture and modern western agriculture that followed is that neither of these methods took into account, natural systems, and how ecosystems function. It appears that in Mesopotamia and Western agriculture, soil and ecosystems are something to be exploited while native cultures learned to revere the soil, plants, and animals, and treated their environment and the planet as 'Mother Earth'.

THE DEVELOPMENT OF MODERN AGRICULTURE

Farming had changed little from Roman times until about 1700, when an agriculture revolution took place. During the 1850's, the industrial revolution spilt over to the farm with the adoption of new mechanised methods which increased crop production and reduced labour. These significant changes were the use of new farm implements which in the mid-1800s were still powered by horses or oxen. The machinery combined with newly developed crop rotations, better use of manure, and improved soil preparation methods lead to a steady increase in crop yield in Europe. From very early times crops were sown by hand by throwing or "broadcasting" the seed, then harvesting the crops by hand or with a scythe. Unfortunately my great-grandfather Nicholas was forced to grow and harvest his wheat crop in the same manner because farming equipment was very rarely available in Australia in the 1860s and if available was extremely expensive because it was imported from England. Nicholas prepared his wheat paddock by digging the soil with a hoe, broadcast the wheat seed by hand, then proceeded to cover the seed with harrows and roll the paddock with a wooden roller constructed from a log. Harvest was done as it has for millennia, by hand with a sickle, followed by drying, stacking and threshing.

A harvester had been invented almost two thousand years previously in Roman times when a crop harvester called the Gallic Vallus was developed in the province of Gaul (modern day France). The machine consisted of a large wooden box, which was carried on two wheels and fitted with rows of

sharp knives at the front edge. The harvester was driven
through the crop by a draught animal, usually a donkey,
pushing from behind; the sharp knives cut the grain heads
which fell into the box where the seed was collected leaving
the stems and straw on the ground. This remarkable machine
is believed to be the earliest mechanical harvester ever to be
invented and was the forerunner to the 'stripper' which was
developed in Australia eighteen hundred years later.

For unknown reasons, the Gallic harvester disappeared
from use in the third century as the Roman Empire collapsed.
But the harvester was reborn in Australia in 1843 when John
Ridley invented a harvesting machine based on the original
Roman Gallic invention from an article, he read about it in the
London Encyclopedia of Agriculture. Ridley did not just
reproduce the Gallic reaper; he also improved the original
design. His design was a wooden box with a comb mounted
in front with rotating beater positioned behind the comb. As
horses pushed the stripper through the crop, the wheat heads
were forced through the comb, removed by the beater and
collected in the storage box. The mixture of grain and chaff
was later separated with a small stationary winnower. The
results were impressive.

My great grandfather Nicholas Seis grew tired of
harvesting his wheat crops by hand – it took him a day to
harvest one acre using a scythe. Seeing the opportunity to
expand his crop area he purchased a 'Ridley Stripper' in the
1880s which allowed him to harvest up to ten acres per day.
Encouraged by the ease of harvest he expanded his wheat
crop to 100 acres.

The development of grain harvesting machines did not
stop with the Ridley Stripper. Thanks to the attempts made by
James Morrow, Victor McKay and a number of other
inventors, a unique stripping combine harvester was
designed and built in Australia. The Australian combine
harvester could strip and thresh ears of wheat, as well as

separate the grain from chaff and straw. These were originally three different jobs requiring three machines, a stripper, thresher and winnower. The combine harvester could harvest 50 acres (20 hectares) a day and be operated by two men. One man drove the horse team and the other filled and unloaded the bags of grain.

In 1895 Hugh Victor McKay started mass producing stripping combine harvesters which he sold under the name "Sunshine Harvester". By 1916 these machines had become very popular and revolutionised the wheat industry in Australia. It was one of these 'Sunshine' Harvesters that Nicholas grandson Harry purchased in the 1930s, allowing him to expand his wheat growing area further.

The advent of steam power and later petrol powered engines brought a whole new outlook to the production of crops. The powered farm implements in the early 1800s were steam engines on wheels that could be used to drive mechanical farm machinery using a large flexible leather belt. The earliest tractors were steam-powered, ploughing engines, which were employed in pairs and positioned on either side of a field, pulling, a plough back and forth between them using a wire cable.

The first petrol-powered tractor was invented and built in 1892 by John Froelich in Iowa USA. This tractor had limited success, but it started the development of the tractor that we use today. These early tractors were not very well accepted by farmers who saw them as expensive, unreliable and not as useful as horse teams, until Henry Ford introduced the first mass-produced tractor, in 1917. They were built in the USA, Ireland, England and Russia, and by 1923, Henry Ford and his Fordson tractor had a significant share of the world tractor market. The very first tractor owned by Harry Seis, was a Fordson which he bought in 1930. Harry saw mechanisation as a great innovation, and his purchase of the Fordson Tractor, Sunshine Harvester, plough and seed drill allowed him to grow over 300 acres of wheat annually.

Since ancient times, crops like wheat, oats and barley have been grown by killing all the plants that may affect the growth of the planted crop. This has traditionally been done by ploughing and has, over thousands of years produced good crop and grain yields, but at the appalling expense of destroying grasslands, creating deserts and saline soils in all corners of the planet.

The adverse effects of too much soil disturbance were most likely started by the Romans over 2000 years ago when they discovered that crop yields could be improved by double ploughing. They, of course, could not have known that the increase in crop yield was achieved at the expense of their soil, and yields were boosted from increased soil nutrients, mineralisation of soil and loss of soil carbon and soil structure.

Many farmers today grow wheat in the same manner my father Harry and farmers of his era did in the 1930s. Harry initially grew crops with horse teams, using the same method taught to him by his father, Joseph. In the period from 1930 to 1990, a well-prepared wheat paddock was one that was ploughed early in the season, cultivated after rainfall events and by crop planting time was weed free, with good soil "tilth"- having no clods or lumps.

The primary purpose of ploughing is to turn over the upper layer of the soil to a depth of up to fifteen centimetres (six inches) and is usually done with a plough with large round discs or blades. Cultivating or tilling is executed after the paddock has been ploughed and is done with a machine call a scarifier or cultivator. These machines have tynes which pass through the soil, breaking up the clods created by the plough. The process of ploughing and cultivating is done to prepare the ground in readiness for planting seeds like wheat or oats by creating loose soil. The method removed weeds and created a good environment for seed germination, but I am very doubtful if it retained soil moisture.

One positive thing about sowing crops in this manner is that it will mineralise nutrients like nitrogen and make them available to the plants. Regrettably, the nitrogen comes at the expense of soil that is depleted in organic carbon. Ploughing to create very fine tilth where the soil particles are made very small with excess cultivation can cause the soil to become hard and compacted, lacking oxygen, and with little ability to absorb water from rainfall. The lack of water and oxygen also causes a reduction in soil microbial diversity which in turn reduces nutrient cycling and plant nutrient availability. The adverse effects of ploughing and cultivating are numerous: erosion, soil compaction, declining soil nutrients, increasing weeds and loss of soil carbon are considered unavoidable and accepted as normal.

Ploughing soil to grow crops created dysfunctional nutrient depleted soil on Winona during the 1940s and the effects were still apparent in the 1990s. Harry was using the best wheat growing techniques available to him, but these methods created soil that became hard, compacted and lifeless, lacking soil carbon and the ability to cycle nutrients. This was associated with declining crop yields and eventually, soil erosion, which created huge gullies through Winona. Unfortunately, there are still many farmers the world over using these same techniques and destroying the world's farming soil.

I was no different to the farmers who preceded me. During the 1980's I continued to grow about three hundred acres of wheat and two hundred acres of oats in the same manner that my father had done since the 1930s. To achieve this, I started ploughing on the first summer rain in November. After six weeks, when the weed seeds had germinated, the area was scarified with an implement designed to break up clods of soil and remove weeds. As more weeds grew the paddocks would be cultivated to remove them and break the soil to a finer tilth. The area would be ploughed scarified and cultivated from four to six times over a six or seven month period before the wheat crop was finally sown in May or June.

The main difference between my father and me was I had a bigger tractor and wider implements that made me more efficient at killing weeds and killing the soil. In other words, I had the potential to destroy Winona twice as fast as my father did.

As well as the problems of reduced soil carbon, declining soil nutrients and soil water availability with the traditional methods I was using to grow wheat, another issue was becoming apparent. A few years earlier, when I was a teenager, my father Harry instructed me to plough a pasture paddock in preparation for sowing a wheat crop. The fact that we were killing good pasture to grow a crop worried my father, who often said that it was terrible that we had to kill pasture and grass to be able to produce a crop of wheat.

With conventional cropping methods, all of the pasture is destroyed so that the crop can be grown. This self-defeating system is also used to grow forage crops to fill an annual stock food shortage. This creates an even larger food shortage the following year because all of the grass and pasture has been killed so the crop can be grown. Growing cereal crops for grain production has the same effect. After the grain is harvested, the paddocks are bare. Not only is there no stock feed in the crop residue because there is no grass but worse, there is no ground- cover. There is no mulch, no litter, no humus and very little life in the soil. The usual answer is to add more fertiliser, which is an accepted farming method around the world, with the only real wealth created, going to fertiliser, seed and chemical companies.

Harry was correct. One of the many problems with killing all of the grass to sow a crop was that it destroyed the pasture that is so essential for livestock production and maintaining the health of the soil. The pasture then had to be re-sown at high expense. Re-sowing pasture was a significant cost in the 1980s as it is today. The cost of re-sowing pastures can cost over one hundred dollars per hectare plus the labour involved.

I thought about my father's comments for many years 'How could we sow crops without killing the grasses?'. The answer came in 1993.

Direct Drilling

An answer to the problems associated with ploughing came in the 1960s when herbicides were first introduced into Australia, and by 1980, as herbicides became more acceptable to use, sowing crops into untilled soil became possible. The weeds that defeated Harry forty years earlier could now be controlled.

The primary herbicide that changed weed control and the manner in which crops are grown was Glyphosate (*N*-(phosphonomethyl)glycine). It was discovered to be herbicide by Monsanto chemist John E. Franz in 1970 and marketed as 'Roundup'. It is a broad-spectrum systemic herbicide used to kill annual broadleaf weeds and grasses that compete with commercial crops.

In my search to find better ways of managing Winona during the late 1980s, I heard about a newly developed technique of drilling or sowing crops without ploughing the soil.

The technique called 'direct drilling' was the forerunner of what is now called zero tillage which is defined as a system of planting (seeding) crops into the untilled soil by opening a narrow slot or trench of sufficient width and depth to obtain proper seed coverage. No other soil tillage such as ploughing or cultivating is done.

This method of sowing crops is a significant step forward because crops can be planted in one pass and with very little soil disturbance. Zero tillage can achieve considerable savings in fuel and labour costs, reduced soil erosion and soil compaction, improved soil water infiltration and greater soil moisture retention, while attaining the same yields as conventional cropping methods where ploughing is used.

To be able to sow crops by 'direct drilling' it is necessary to use a seed drill with narrow and strong sowing points that are designed for penetrating hard, unploughed soil.

In 1989 I owned an old Massey seed drill, which I converted to direct drill seeding by simply bolting narrow seeding points onto the existing tynes. I started sowing small areas of oats for sheep feed. This worked reasonably well even though the drill and tynes were never designed to work in conditions that were not ploughed. The results were encouraging enough to know it would work with a better seed drill. I also owned a newer 'Connor Shea' drill that had stronger tynes and frame. I converted that machine to a direct drill seeder and achieved results that were equal in grain yield to my traditionally ploughed paddocks.

During the early days of 'direct drilling crops,' it was important to kill all grass with herbicide for up to six months pre-sowing. To achieve good grain yields I used Glyphosate. The first weed control treatment being in December, another in February, and another in late April before the crop was planted. After the crop had emerged, I used another herbicide for broadleaf weeds then a different herbicide for grass weed control. I was using five to six herbicide applications plus an insecticide.

Thinking I could further increase the grain yield and make more profit I sought agronomy advice on what I should do. Following the recommendation I received, I tested the soil for nutrients and was advised to increase the rate of fertiliser by forty percent, which was to be applied during crop planting time. To maintain crop yields, I was also told to add nitrogen to the crop, during the year.

I was using one hundred kilograms per hectare of Diammonium phosphate (DAP) which is a commonly used fertiliser used around the world for supplying nitrogen and phosphorus. The recommended increase in fertiliser had the potential to be toxic to wheat crops because of the high amount of nitrogen. To address this problem, I would need to modify the seed drill so that the DAP was split and placed at two levels, half with the seed and the other half deeper so the wheat plant could access it as it grew. Fortunately, I did not take this advice. I thought that there was something wrong if I needed to apply so much fertiliser that it had the potential to kill the plants, so I began to investigate.

For all of the great advantages of using zero tillage technology, I was still using many of the ground preparation processes with zero tillage that had been used for the last 200 years with traditional farming methods. Instead of ploughing and cultivating the soil five to six times, now I was killing the weeds that supposedly threaten the wheat crop, with five to six chemical herbicide applications proudly supplied, at great expense, by multinational companies. The herbicide, insecticide and increased fertiliser applications were changing the soil ecology which prevented much of the natural soil building processes and nutrient cycling. It was the destruction of the soil ecosystem that was making it necessary to add more fertiliser.

These direct drill methods had prevented many of the erosion problems, improved the soil structure and increased water infiltration on Winona but still had not addressed many of the soil health concerns. The pesticide application and increased fertiliser were also adding a very significant cost to growing crops, and I felt the only people making money from growing crops were the suppliers and manufacturers of fertiliser and pesticides.

In other words, I replaced the plough with a boom spray and herbicides but had not changed the fundamental philosophy of farming.

❧ 4 ❧

PASTURE CROPPING

Daryl Cluff and his wife Loraine own the property Olive Lodge which is about half an hour drive from Winona on the western side of Barneys Reef. I had known Daryl or 'Cluffy', for many years, having played a lot of cricket against him. Cricket, as we played it in the 'bush', was 'out of the ordinary', and although most people played to win the game, it was played in a very social manner. There were no turf pitches in that era; the cricket pitches were made from the nests of ants, which are locally called meat ants. The large ant nests were dug with picks and shovels, with furious ants still in them, loaded on a truck, and transported to a suitable paddock, which was often owned by one of the members of the local cricket team. The remains of the ant nest were mixed with water to a suitable consistency and spread and levelled like concrete to form a hard pitch. Before playing the cricket match, the pitch was covered with a green matting cover that vaguely resembled very coarse grass.

These pitches last for many years, with some more than fifty years old and still being used. Bush or country cricket has been played on these types of pitches for at least a century.

In the Gulgong area during the 1970s and 1980s there were eight teams, most of which had ant bed wickets in someone's paddock. The cricket games were great fun and usually started with someone armed with a broom sweeping the sheep and kangaroo droppings off the pitch and ended with copious amounts of beer, with no one even remembering who won the game.

It was during one of these cricket matches that I first met Cluffy, who played for a small village called Birriwa, which was near his farm; I played for the Gulgong Unquenchables, which was appropriately named after our beer drinking talents.

During the early 1990s, Cluffy was appointed the local Landcare coordinator, and many of the duties of his job were to supervise Landcare projects like tree planting and restoring saline areas. Some of these projects were on Winona, and consequently, Cluffy would occasionally visit the Landcare sites. We had both changed many of our traditional agriculture methods by planting trees, restoring saline areas, and changed our crop growing methods to direct drilling.

Cluffy arrived one day in April and inspected the Landcare projects, and then we settled into drinking a few beers and discussing the problems of the world. It was one such evening after many beers that it was said "Why can't we direct drill crops into the perennial native red grass? Why do we need to kill the grass to sow wheat if it is not actively growing at the same time as the crop?

Red Grass (bothriochloa macra) is a warm season perennial grass that grows in the warmer summer months from October to March. It slows its growth as the weather cools to become fully dormant from May until late September. Cereal crops like wheat and oats are planted from April to May and grow through the dormant period of the red grass. Most of Australia's warm season or C4 grass species have a dormant winter period like red grass.

Pasture Cropping was born.

The beer drinking evening was in late April 1993. There had already been a frost, and the red grass had begun its dormant phase. It was a perfect time to try our insane idea. I was using Glyphosate to kill weeds, including red grass, when I was direct drilling crops, but this time I was focused on paddocks that had no herbicide application previously applied. The paddock had its usual amount of non-productive annual weeds like capeweed, Patterson's Curse, silver grass, and ryegrass as well as about ten percent warm season native perennial grass, most of which was red grass. If I were to achieve any grain yield from my experiment, the weeds would need to be killed, but I thought a lower amount of Glyphosate should not harm the red grass after the frost. The recommended rate of Glyphosate was two litres per hectare; I believed that one litre per hectare would kill the weeds but not affect the dormant red grass.

Within two weeks of our beer drinking evening, I had sprayed the weeds with herbicide and was sowing a crop of oats using my direct drill seeder. Meanwhile, Cluffy had also planted a crop of wheat using the same techniques. My oat crop germinated like a typically sown crop, but it was hard to see the small oat seedlings amongst the dry dormant grass and dead weeds. It was the most untidy oat crop I had ever seen, but I thought it might produce feed for the sheep. As the season progressed, the crop started to look more impressive as the green oat plants grew above the litter and dry grass. By October the oats had grown to about a metre high, then during November the crop was harvested and achieved an excellent grain yield of three tonnes per hectare. What I thought may be merely a low-cost, easy method of growing sheep feed turned out to be much more than that. The crop produced around the same yield as my traditionally sown crops. The red grass that was dormant when the paddock was sprayed with herbicide was not only unharmed but thriving, growing vigorously out of the oat stubble after the crop was harvested.

Not having a lot of confidence whether it would work a second year I sowed most of my wheat and oat crops using precise herbicide weed control and decided to Pasture Crop a small area of fifty acres to wheat as well as fifty acres to oats. The Pasture Cropped paddocks yielded the same as the direct drill crops. This was enough evidence for me, and I changed all of my crops to Pasture Crop the following year and have not sown a crop in any other way since.

With the technique working so well we thought we should name it something. We were struggling to find an appropriate name until one evening at Olive Lodge while drinking many of Cluffy's famous homebrews Cluffy suggested the name 'Pasture Cropping' and the rest is history.

The beer drinking evening that saw the birth of Pasture Cropping was not the only evening Cluffy and I had drinking beer and coming up with ideas. Something as radical as sowing crops into perennial grass attracts a lot of critics and very little encouragement. We were on our own with everyone telling us we were not only wrong but mad. Our constant communication tempered with evenings discussing new ideas over beer was necessary because we had no support from anyone - just criticism.

Anyone that has done anything new or different knows that it is not easy putting up with constant criticism, so I started to seek some scientific advice, but all the scientists and agronomists I approached showed no interest. In 1996 this was to change. That year a group of farmers from the north of the state came to Winona. Leading that group was Dr Christine Jones, who became very excited by the Pasture Cropping concept and could immediately see the potential in what we were doing.

Dr Christine Jones is an internationally renowned and highly respected groundcover and soils ecologist with a PhD in Soil Biochemistry. Christine was the only scientist who supported what we were doing and is a major part of the Pasture Cropping evolution. I would often phone Christine and inform her of the latest developments and questioned why some things were working and others not. Because of Christine's ecological background and thorough understanding of soil, she solved many of the problems and became very supportive throughout the development years, as well as continuing to be supportive today.

Examples of people being narrow-minded and not wanting to understand are numerous, but one stands out. In October 1997 a field day was organised at Winona, and about fifty curious and mostly critical people arrived, headed by a well-known agronomist. With everyone standing in a good wheat crop that was estimated to yield three tonnes per hectare the agronomist had instructed everyone to look for crop diseases. In his opinion, there had to be a disease because a large amount of the green perennial grass growing amongst the wheat had to promote disease in the crop. Upon finding no crop disease, the general comment was that I must have been lucky. Everyone overlooked the fact that it was possible to grow a good wheat crop into the perennial grass, and started searching for problems that were not there. They ignored the reasons why there was no disease and the benefit of having native perennial grass beneath the wheat. After that day I realised that I was on my own and could not expect anything but criticism from most agronomists and scientists.

Harry was one of the few people that were supportive. He knew Pasture Cropping would work because it was very similar to the methods he used to grow crops in the 1940s and it solved the riddle of how to grow crops without destroying the pasture and grassland.

After harvesting the second Pasture Cropped paddocks I again noticed that the perennial native grass was much thicker and healthier amongst the crop stubble in both the oat and wheat crops. I contacted Cluffy, and he had seen the same phenomenon. The grass was much better where the crop had been sown than the same grass in the adjoining paddocks. On closer inspection of the area, I noticed that many perennial grass seedlings had germinated in the drill row where the cereal crop had been growing. I had not sown any seed other than the oat crop, so something had stimulated germination of the native perennial grass seed that had lain dormant in the soil for many years. Our low-cost and easy method of sowing crops was turning out to be far more interesting than we thought. Traditional methods of sowing crops kill all competing plants during the crop growing process; this destroys the grassland or pasture in that area. The elimination of the grassland significantly contributes to soil erosion and soil health decline and changes the soil ecosystem. What Pasture Cropping had the potential to do was to not only maintain the existing grassland but to enhance the grassland and even restore it close to the original species diversity.'

WEEDS

Weeds are a problem that has plagued agriculture for hundreds if not thousands of years. Over the centuries they have been controlled mechanically with cultivation and in more recent times with herbicide. Neither of these methods addresses the cause of the weed problem, and often create conditions in which they thrive.

Having seen that Pasture Cropping could work well, I started to search for methods that would improve it and consistently grow crops for grain.

Weeds dominated Winona during this time, and it was important to control them if I was going to grow high yielding grain crops. Controlling weeds in a Pasture Cropping system was not going to be easy because it was essential to keep the perennial grass species alive and suppress annual weeds that affected crop growth.

I started experimenting with different herbicides and searching for advice on what herbicides to use, but most agronomists did not understand why I would want to keep the grass alive. Again I was on my own. I had to find herbicide that would control weeds but not kill the perennial grass. I started to doubt if the Glyphosate herbicide I was using was suitable. I noticed paddocks that were previously Pasture Cropped contained good species diversity of native summer grass, but very few native winter grass species. The reason for this was the summer grass species were going into winter dormancy as Glyphosate was being applied but the cool season, winter grass species were still actively growing, and Glyphosate was killing them. I was unintentionally selecting for a summer growing grassland, and very soon Winona would have very few or no winter species if I continued with that herbicide. I started to search for herbicide that would keep both the summer and winter perennial grass species alive and would kill annual weed species. The one I found was paraquat, which is a non-selective herbicide that kills annual weeds, and with recommended rates will not kill mature perennial plant species. Paraquat acts in the presence of light to desiccate the green parts of all plants with which it comes into contact, so it does not kill plant roots. It was first manufactured and sold in early 1962, becoming popular around the world as a knockdown herbicide in broadacre cropping during the early 1980s, and became available in Australia in 1986. It appeared that I had found the ideal herbicide until I realised that paraquat is one of the most dangerous poisonous herbicides available. It was kind to perennial grass but had the potential to kill humans. I reluctantly used it anyway because I couldn't find anything else which suited my purposes.

I had learned that it was important to use basic agronomy

principals that had been developed for zero-till cropping methods. Weed control was the most important of these. I was continually searching for herbicides that would do as little damage as possible to the existing perennial grass species and still control weeds. I discovered most herbicides that are used when the crop was growing did not kill perennial grass species, but could be used to control annual weeds that were affecting the crop. This gave the potential to increase crop yields, but it did not address my aims of eventually using any chemicals at all.

I needed to understand the reason weeds grow.

Most weeds that compete with crops are annual colonising plants. Annual plants are opportunistic and take advantage of disturbed and bare soil. They have evolved to colonise bare ground and play a valuable role in their natural environment. In grassland, annual plants colonise disturbed sites after soil disturbance from animals and fire. An annual plant has one main reason for living, which is to produce enough seed so the next generation can grow and survive the following year. The method used to grow crops for millennia has been to create disturbed bare soil to advantage the annual crop. Unfortunately, bare soil produced for the crop also creates a perfect environment for other annual plants that we call weeds. It is the method itself that creates weeds, which can be more effectively managed with total ground cover, not bare soil.

Weeds can be managed in a very cost-efficient manner with 'litter' or ground cover. If the litter is placed on the soil surface to produce one hundred percent ground cover of thick mulch, weeds usually do not germinate. Controlling weeds in this manner has been known for centuries and have been used on small farms and gardens for a very long time by applying straw as mulch.

I had been focusing on creating ground cover since the Winona fire in 1979. The extra ground cover encouraged germination of native grass species, and as native grass increased, it created more ground cover. As ground cover increased, it eventually became 40-50 mm thick. With that thickness of litter, not as many weeds germinated and in the mid-1990s I decided to try to measure the changes that I observed by placing some monitoring sites called transects on Winona. The monitoring sites have turned out to be invaluable. The transects showed that as the litter and soil health improved, annual weeds disappeared. The monitoring also confirmed that my observations about Pasture Cropping stimulating native grass seedlings were correct. After a paddock was Pasture Cropped the monitoring sites showed the perennial grass plant numbers increased by as much as fifty-four percent and weeds decreased by as much as sixty-five percent in one year. The increase in perennial grass and decrease in weeds occurred every time a crop was Pasture Cropped into a paddock.

Over time Mother Nature was solving the weed problem for me. As the soil ecosystem started to find a natural balance, I was seeing fewer weeds, not only pre-planting but also while the crop was growing. Part of the reason for this was the thick litter and mulch prevented germination of annual weeds, but the other was a change in soil chemistry. There were a lot of things happening that did not make sense when looking through conventional agronomy eyes.

INSECTS

The thick litter and improving soil allowed me to reduce the amount of herbicide used, but I also had other problems to solve. Insect attack on crops and pastures are a major issue worldwide, and it was no different on Winona. Harry began seeing insects like red legged earth mite and blue oat mite destroy crops and pastures in the 1950s and had very successfully controlled the insects with an insecticide called DDT. When DDT was banned in Australia in 1987 other insecticides became available which I routinely applied because I knew that the crop was going to be attacked by insects. I became concerned about spraying insecticides because it was killing all insects, including beneficial insects as well as native and introduced bees. The scientific advice received was that if I did not control insects with an insecticide, the crop would be destroyed, and the numbers of harmful insects would continue to increase until they became unmanageable. It was implied that if I did not wage war on pests, they would take over Winona.

What would happen if I did not use an insecticide? I decided to try not using it in 1998 when I noticed a large number of insects in an oat crop. Thinking the 50-acre paddock would be utterly destroyed I nervously watched as they started devouring the oat plants. What occurred was not Armageddon, or very much damage at all. The insects ate patches from the crop about 20 meters in diameter then stopped. The oat crop recovered and went on to be no different to the areas without insect damage. On inspection of the areas, I noticed numerous other insects and spiders eating the plant-damaging red-legged earth mites. I had discovered that more diversity of insects and higher numbers of insects was required on Winona, not fewer insects. As the ecosystem on Winona found a natural balance, the invading insect population declined as predators moved in and helped create a balance between insects causing damage and naturally occurring beneficial insects. Insect eaters like spiders, predatory wasps, and lady beetles are needed to control crop-damaging insects. From that time I have not used any insecticides or had any insect damage on Winona.

This was validated in 2007 when University student Elise Wenden did a study on Winona and discovered that Winona had 600% more insects and 135% more insect diversity on Pasture Cropped paddocks when compared to paddocks that were traditionally sown to crops.

A section of Elise Wenden's report reads:

The comparison of different tillage regimes on two properties north of Gulgong, New South Wales, shows significant impacts of conventional tillage and 'Pasture Crop' practices on soil biological populations and diversity.

Pasture Cropping resulted in increased levels of soil biology associated with increased groundcover.

Additional benefits of Pasture Cropping include better soil structure associated with increased soil porosity, which in turn creates habitat for soil microbiology to benefit other predatory organisms. Consequently, Pasture Cropping can be seen as a regenerative tool for sustainable agriculture.

Fertiliser

In the late 1990s, I was concerned about the amount of fertiliser that I was applying when sowing crops. The cost of using one hundred kilograms per hectare of DAP was limiting profit, and I was concerned about what the fertiliser was doing to the soil ecosystem.

I noticed when a wheat crop was sown into paddocks that had scattered perennial grass plants the wheat was growing much better in the crown of the dormant grass. This is contrary to agronomic advice where grass will negatively affect the growth of wheat plants. I was seeing a positive effect of up to fifty percent increase in wheat growth, amongst the perennial plants and found that as perennial grass became denser crop yield increased. I was not sure why I was achieving better crops, but I decided to reduce the fertiliser to eighty kilograms per hectare. To my surprise, there was no difference in grain yield.

The agronomy advice was if I reduced fertiliser rates I would get a reduction in crop and grain yield and the soil would eventually become depleted in nutrients. Against all agronomy recommendations, I cut the fertiliser to sixty kilograms the following year and continued to reduce the fertiliser every year, finding that forty kilograms per hectare were giving the same grain yield as one hundred kilograms per hectare.

I tried seeking information on why this was possible. No one knew, and very few people were interested, saying that I must be wrong or lying about the crop yields. I found the answer from Dr Christine Jones. The perennial grass plants that had been increasing in numbers and species diversity had been improving soil structure, water holding capacity, soil organic matter and soil carbon. Coupled with this was a vast increase in soil microbes and soil microbe diversity.

This information was also confirmed with a study done by Dr Peter Ampt & Sarah Doornbos from Sydney University in December 2010 which showed soil microbe numbers had doubled and associated soil carbon and total nitrogen had also doubled.

In 2011 Dr Christine Jones and I became curious about what was happening in the soil and collected samples to 60 cm. These showed an average increase in all nutrients of 160% and also showed double soil carbon

CROP DISEASE

Crop disease is a severe problem for producers worldwide. Fungal diseases like 'take all' and Rhizoctonia root rot is an ongoing challenge because they can damage and kill plants which in turn will severely affect grain yield. During Harry's era, and the early part of my farming life, crops were often severely affected by disease. Today there are options for control of many of these diseases, but Harry did not have any alternative and had to accept the loss. Some farmers today use crop rotations and the removal of plants that host the disease, with herbicides pre-crop planting, while others rely on fungicides. A severe consequence of using fungicides is they alter and impact soil microbial communities which can trigger a change of the soil food web making fungal disease worse over time. Crop disease is a symptom of the way crops are grown, and disease is often a result of biologically unhealthy soil that has an imbalance of soil microorganisms, with microbes that naturally control the disease being in too small numbers to control the disease-causing organism effectively. If the soil ecosystem is restored and has a diverse range of soil microbes, crop disease is rarely a problem.

As more perennial grass species returned to Winona and the soil improved, disease in crops declined and now does not occur. Fungicides are no longer required and have not been used on crops or as a seed dressing since 1998. The improvement in the ecosystem was validated with a soil microbial count done at Dr Elaine Ingham's laboratory in Bangalow NSW. The total fungi on Winona had increased by 862%; protozoa by 640%, bacteria by 350% and nematodes increased by over 1000%. People that have crops attacked by nematodes would be shocked by a massive increase in nematodes, but in this case, the increase was from beneficial nematodes.

DEVELOPMENT YEARS

The development years of Pasture Cropping through the 1990s were times that experienced good rainfall, and the effects of this were excellent grain yield and grassland improvement. The Pasture Crop oats produced up to 4 tonnes per hectare of grain, and most crops yielded about the same as the district average of two to three tonnes per hectare. During this time I had not experienced a dry year with less than average rainfall. How would the crop perform during a dry year? Unfortunately, I got my wish multiplied by ten. The new century would produce the ten driest years since my great grandfather experienced the Federation drought, exactly 100 years earlier.

The many critics continued to say that I was not conserving soil moisture and could not possibly grow a crop without killing the grass before sowing the crop. For at least 100 years in Australia and most other countries, it was and still is necessary to prepare paddocks months in advance by ploughing or killing weeds with herbicides. The rationale behind this was twofold. The weeds would remove soil moisture and nutrients that were necessary for the soon to be planted crop. The paddock required removal of anything growing and the soil had to be bare with no weeds that may use the precious water intended for crop growth.

These methods of paddock preparation left the soil bare for many months pre-sowing, leaving the soil exposed to the extremes of temperature, wind and water. Another problem with this method is that the unprotected soil also leaves soil microorganisms exposed to extremes of heat and cold. A soil surface temperature of 60 degrees centigrade will kill most soil microorganisms, which has been demonstrated by Tim Wiley from the Western Australia Department of Agriculture who did some research work on this subject. He showed that simple ground cover of litter and perennial grass reduced the extremes of heat and cold on the soil

The results show that ground cover keeps the soil cooler in summer and actively growing perennials moderate the microclimate even further. The bare soil was up to 30 C hotter than the perennial grass plots (i.e. a maximum of 33 C compared to 63 C). Litter and perennial grass cover also protected the grass from extremes of cold weather. These differences in soil temperature have significant implications for soil biology and health. -Tim Wiley 2nd April 2003

Tim Wiley demonstrated a very important fact. Bare soil and associated extremes of temperature will kill soil microbes. Without soil microorganisms, the soil becomes dysfunctional, reducing nutrient cycling, nutrient availability and water availability. The plants growing in paddocks before a crop is sown are believed to use soil water, and of course they do, but how much moisture is lost to evaporation, and how many soil microbes are killed by having bare soil exposed to the elements?

When Pasture Cropping in drought years, with less than ideal rainfall, I found that grain yields were no smaller than traditional cropping methods. This again was puzzling until, after doing soil tests on soil carbon, it became apparent that Winona's soil carbon levels were increasing. One of the early soil carbon comparisons was done in 2004 by Van Bushby, a retired CSIRO scientist, who recorded that Winona soil had almost double total organic carbon andthe soil also had almost double water holding capacity as a result. The relevance of improved water holding capacity when soil carbon is increased becomes apparent when Dr Christine Jones explains the science.

An increase of 16.8 litres (almost two buckets) of extra plant available water could be stored per square metre in the top 30 cm (12") of soil with a bulk density of 1.4 g/cm3, for every 1% increase in the level of soil organic carbon. This equates to 168,000 litres of water that could be stored per hectare, in addition to the water-holding capacity of the soil itself.

The flip side is that the same amount of water-holding capacity will be lost when soil carbon levels fall. Low soil moisture and low levels of soil organic carbon go hand in hand.

Soil organic carbon levels in many areas have fallen by at least 3% (in absolute terms) since the time of European settlement, This reduction in soil carbon content represents the LOSS of the ability of soil to store around 504,000 litres of water per hectare. (Dr Christine Jones).

The only practical method of increasing soil carbon is with plants. Lots of plants. Winona's plants were starting to increase at an astounding rate as the grassland was resurrected. This coupled with sowing a crop into the perennial grassland added to the plant diversity and rapidly increased soil carbon.

Winona was starting to increase its inbuilt water storage system.

When Nicholas Seis and the early Australian explorers looked in awe at the Australian grasslands, they could not have known about the potential of Mother Nature to solve many problems. As Australia's grassland grew, it added organic matter and root exudates to the soil. Over thousands of years the grassland and associated soil microbes were increasing the soil carbon to very high levels as shown by Sir Paul Edmund Strzelecki in the 1840s. Nicholas' Round Camp grasslands could have had 5-6 % organic carbon. This grassland soil had the potential to store over a half million litres of water per hectare and replenish it every time it rained. This is partly why Australia's grassland and the world prairies and savannas were so productive and had nurtured native people and millions of native animals for many thousands of years.

Van Busby's results encouraged me to look closely at what else was happening on Winona and his results stimulated interest with Australia's leading scientific and research organisation the CSIRO.

Led by Dr Mark Howden and Sarah Bruce a research project was conducted on Winona from September 2003 to January 2005. It was funded and supported by CSIRO Sustainable Ecosystems. Sections of Sarah Bruce's Paper are quoted below:

Anecdotal reports of the benefits of pasture-cropping, such as: increasing soil cover, increasing biomass production, and reductions in soil acidity and transient waterlogging, prompted more detailed investigations of the impacts of 'Pasture Cropping' on biomass production, cover, soil nitrogen and water compared to more conventional cropping and grazing enterprises. This study examined the general impacts of Pasture Cropping on biomass production, ground cover, soil water, and nitrogen compared to a C4 dominant perennial pasture and a direct-drilled winter oats crop in a replicated field experiment in the central-west wheat-belt of NSW.

A field experiment was conducted to determine the effect of Pasture Cropping on biomass production, total ground cover, soil water and soil potentially available nitrogen compared to more conventional cropping and grazing enterprises.

Pasture Cropping with native deep-rooted perennial grasses is one of the most promising innovations to reduce waterlogging and water tables resulting from high rainfall seasons. Native perennial pastures have evolved to grow in the weathered and often saline soils of Australia, show a considerable band of pH tolerance (Johnston et al. 2001) and are persistent if appropriate management practices are used. Pasture Cropping is one such system used by farmers in Australian farming systems, and involves direct-drilling winter crops (C3) into predominantly summer growing pastures (mostly C4 species). In comparison with C3 species, C4 species grow at higher temperatures and are more efficient in their use of water. From an ecological perspective, the key feature of this system is that there is a separation of the growing seasons of the crop and pasture with only limited overlapping 'shoulder' periods when competition is likely. This differs from other intercropping systems where growth tends to be more synchronous. The summer C4 pastures replace the fallow of typical cropping systems. What might this seasonal separation of resource use mean in terms of biomass production, water balance, and erosion?

Conclusion

The separation of C3 and C4 growing periods and the mix of shallow-rooted and deep-rooted plants in the pasture-crop treatment have a number of potential benefits compared to conventional cropping pasture management practices. In comparison with traditional cropping practices, Pasture Cropping leads to higher total ground cover year-round and increased total biomass outside of the cropping season. This year-round increase in ground cover and growth is likely to result in reduced wind and water erosion, reduced weed outbreaks and increases in soil organic matter. Pasture Cropping may reduce the likelihood of water-logging, dryland salinity, loss of Nitrogen through denitrification, and soil acidification developing. In an era when water-logging, dryland salinity, soil acidification and loss of soil carbon are having deleterious impacts on the productivity and sustainability of farming enterprises, Pasture Cropping may provide one option for addressing these problems.

The research results showed promising results from the data collected but only touched on the surface of the potential of the Pasture Cropping technique.

PROBLEMS

As with anything new and different it was not always smooth sailing, there were obstacles along the way, but the development of 'pasture cropping' continued.

I had adopted planned grazing and had the adult sheep on Winona in one mob of about 2500 ewes and 1500 hoggets under one-year-old in another mob. Fewer mobs and larger mobs managed in rotation around Winona allowed plants to recover before re-grazing, favoured perennial species and Pasture Cropping stimulated the recruitment of many different native species. The grassland was starting to return, and after good summer rain, the grass grew over a meter tall. I found the crop that was planted into this much grass, even after it had become dormant at the start of winter, did not perform well and grain yield was reduced. The significantly improved grassland was starting to create a problem. After discussion with Dr Christine Jones, we thought that the tall and thick grass might be affecting the crop in three ways. The emerging crop was being shaded, making it slow to develop. The second problem encountered was that the large amount of dry grass had created a temporary nitrogen deficiency which also had the potential to affect crop performance.

A temporary reduction of plant available nitrogen can occur from immobilisation (tie-up) of soil nitrogen. When soil microbes are decomposing high carbon-low nitrogen residues, such as dry grass residue or wheat straw, they need more nitrogen to digest the material that is present in the residue. Immobilisation occurs when Nitrate (NO_3^--N) and / or Ammonium (NH_4^+-N) present in the soil is used by the living microbes to build proteins. Once the dry grass has become highly decayed, immobilisation of nitrogen stops, and mineralisation starts. In other words, when the dry grass is being broken down by microbes there can be a temporary nitrogen deficiency for the newly established crop. When the dry grass is fully decomposed, there is a net gain of nitrogen which is available to the crop later in the crop growing season.

The third unseen problem was related to the perennial grass roots which were competing with the emerging crop for nutrients and water. All three problems could be solved at the same time. Much of the tall grass and associated root mass needed to be removed. The usual method of removing excess material would be to burn it, but the grass litter was a great asset which controlled weeds and added organic matter to the soil. I wanted to mulch the grass onto the soil surface. An answer could be to mulch it with a mower or slasher mechanically, but this takes time and cost money. The obvious remedy to this was to use the large mob of sheep to eat and trample the tall grass. I learned, by using a large mob of 2500 sheep for three to four days in fifteen to twenty-hectare paddocks, that much of the grass and associated material was eaten and trampled onto the ground. But this was not enough to reduce the material sufficiently to Pasture Crop the paddock without blocking the seed drill with dry grass. This problem was solved by grazing the area again three weeks later, immediately before sowing the crop, this time with excellent results. The sheep consumed much of the dry grass and the remainder mulched onto the ground. The addition of manure and urine from the sheep was a great bonus which added nutrients that were available to the soon to be planted crop.

I found that grazing in this manner had the following benefits. It controlled many of the weeds with sheep eating the plants, and the thick litter that the animals pushed onto the ground created thick mulch and prevented most weeds germinating. The pulse of nutrients from manure and urine from the sheep was a significant supply of natural fertiliser for the crop which allowed me to reduce fertiliser even further and obtain better crop yields. The grazing opened the canopy of the grassland; allowing light to penetrate and prevented the emerging crop being shaded by tall grass. The removal of much of the dry plant material by sheep also helped reduce soil nitrogen depletion by turning the dry plant material into manure. Most importantly, the removal of green plant material also pruned the plant roots, which lessened sub-surface competition for water and nutrients and added very valuable organic matter and nutrients to the soil as the roots decomposed.

The stoppage of plant root growth by grazing plants has been shown by research work that Franklin. J. Crider from the United States Department of agriculture did in 1954. The results of his work have been included in the grazing section of this book, but Crider also obtained some interesting data that would turn out to be beneficial for Pasture Cropping many years later.

Crider proved that grazing perennial plants short and repeatedly would weaken and stress the plant. He also demonstrated that root mass could be reduced by as much as 800% with repeated grazing. However, with Pasture Cropping, where an annual crop is being planted into perennial grass plants, this type of grazing could be used to deliberately stress and weaken the perennial plants and benefit the newly emerging sown crop. The weakened perennial plant would be less able to compete with the crop seedling which would allow the annual crop to grow more vigorously and lessen the need to kill the grass plant with herbicides or ploughing. The plant roots that have been reduced by 800% are no longer alive and are being turned into organic matter by soil microbes, improving soil structure and adding nutrients for the crop to use. The six to eight-month period while the crop is growing will allow ample time for the grass to fully recover before re-grazing after the crop is harvested for grain.

I had previously observed an improvement in crop performance after the grassland was heavily grazed but a combination of Dr Christine Jones' advice and the results of Crider's research demonstrated the importance of reducing perennial plant biomass. It has also shown why some Pasture Cropping practitioners sometimes get less than favourable results when Pasture Cropping into tall grass. I cannot express enough the importance of reducing the plant's biomass by grazing at least two or three times, and one or two months before crop planting time.

SOIL STRUCTURE

Grazing animals and growing crops on the same farm has been practised for centuries, but in the last 20 – 30 years sheep and cattle have been removed from zero-till cropping programs around the world because of the belief that animals cause soil compaction and reduce crop yield. Nearly all soil compaction problems are human-made and are symptoms of the cropping methods being used.

Sheep and cattle could be described as one pass mowing, mulching and fertilising machines. Animals are an essential asset and can be used to eat weeds, create litter and ground cover, cycle nutrients by turning plant material into plant-available nutrients and increase income and profit. On Winona where I use large mobs of sheep to prepare a paddock to Pasture Crop, soil compaction is not a problem. This is because there is a thick mulch layer to protect the soil surface and a dense fibrous root system beneath the soil surface from the perennial grass roots. It is a lack of ground cover and plant root mass beneath the soil surface that causes soil compaction, not animals.

During the early experimental years of Pasture Cropping, I learned that crops sown into hard compacted soil with poor soil structure were slow to establish and crop performance was also poor. This is not unique to Pasture Cropping. Most crops, sown with zero till methods, struggle to yield well when planted into soil with inferior soil structure. In Australia and many other countries worldwide, poor soil structure is a legacy of past farming and grazing practices, created by cultivating the soil and continuous grazing. My short-term fix to this problem was to develop a seed drill with strong tynes and narrow points that could penetrate the soil relatively deeply and easily, but not create any side disturbance. This created loose soil under the seed and improved the infiltration of water. I also discovered that disc seeders, on hard soil, did not give satisfactory results. However, when soil structure and soil health improves disc seeders can produce excellent results and have many advantages over tyne drills.

For a few years, the drill I was using to sow the crops was simply an old seed drill that I had converted by removing half the tynes and bolting narrow seeding points onto the remaining ones. This drill worked well as long as the soil was wet, but as the grassland species and associated litter increased, the old drill could not pass through the litter without acting like a rake and blocking with dry grass. To solve this problem I thought I should purchase a new one, but seed drills are expensive and not having sufficient money to buy a new seed drill I looked at constructing my own.

My father purchased an international scarifier in 1974. It had been used as a secondary tillage implement to remove weeds and break up the large clods left by the initial ploughing, but now the disused and rusting old machine with two flat tyres was sitting behind a shed. It had reasonably strong tynes, and I could see the potential of resuscitating the now obsolete scarifier and giving it a new life as a seed drill, specifically for Pasture Cropping. Fortunately my cousin Doug Seis is an excellent welder and engineer, so I gave him the job of converting the old machine.

Some of the tynes were removed and the remaining ones spaced twelve inches apart. At the front of the machine, fine steel discs called coulters were mounted to cut through the heavy grass mulch and into the soil. The coulter openings make way for a narrow point, which parts the soil with minimal disturbance and creates a space for seeds. A trailer attached to the rear of the seeder, called an air cart, was built to hold and distribute the seed and fertiliser which is pushed by air through hoses and deposited into the slot cut by the narrow points.

A pump and tank from a discarded spray unit were mounted on the seeder to distribute liquid compost tea and worm leachate directly into the drill row with the seed. Lastly, a seedbox was attached on the back of the drill to allow for sowing smaller seeds like forage brassica, tillage radish, and millet for multi-species crops.

After the air seeder deposits the grain, fertiliser and compost tea into the narrow incision, a bank of press wheels run along each seeded line, gently compressing the surface to ensure that the grain is held closely by the soil, thereby increasing germination rates.

I now had a machine that could plant multiple crop species simultaneously. It would allow me to reduce fertiliser by over seventy percent and use liquid products like worm leachate or compost tea and apply them all in one pass through very thick litter.

One of the problems I had may seem simple, but was an issue for me at the time, and can be for people adopting Pasture Cropping now.

When I was growing crops in the 1970s and 1980s, the paddocks were ploughed and cultivated up to six times which took a lot of work and needed many days to complete. With this amount of ploughing and cultivating it was necessary to work at night. Many farmers of that era and today work throughout the night and often have shifts with farmworkers to continue twenty-four hours of the day. This was necessary to get the job done quickly but was also very expensive, with large amounts of diesel being consumed, as well as wear and tear on tractors, machinery and people.

When I changed the ground preparation methods and started using large mobs of sheep to prepare the paddock instead of ploughing I had reduced my time needed driving the tractor by at least eighty percent, and it was no longer a requirement to work at night.

This was a great saving in time, labour, tractor hours and money, but as I watched the lights of tractors working through the evening, I felt guilty and thought that I should have been working as the neighbours were. Surprisingly this was one of the more difficult things I had to overcome.

But I hasten to add that I no longer have pangs of guilt as I watch tractor lights turning in ever diminishing circles while ploughing at night, unnecessarily burning diesel and destroying soil while I enjoy a cold beer.

What Has Happened On Winona?

One of the most frequent comments about Pasture Cropping is how it improves the existing pasture that the crop is sown into. The improvement is seen with the better growth of plants and, more importantly, an increase in perennial grass numbers that have germinated from seed which has lain dormant, sometimes for many years. This phenomenon has been reported in all states of Australia and other countries around the world, andhas tremendous potential. Not only can crops be grown without destroying the grassland or pasture, but the technique has the potential for restoring grasslands and grassland species around the world.

I was beginning to doubt whether soil disturbance was the only factor influencing the perennial grass seedling recruitment after a crop has been Pasture Cropped. Soil disturbance by ploughing and cultivation had not stimulated perennial grass germination ever before on Winona, so what was different this time?

It has been observed on Winona, and by Pasture Cropping practitioners, where crop planting procedures are done without sowing grain, no grass recruitment is seen. This first happened to me accidentally when I had forgotten to fill the seed drill with oats, and some of the sowing was done without grain. Where the crop had grown there was good recruitment of perennial grass and where there was no crop growing no grass recruitment had occurred. The annual crop plants were somehow stimulating the perennial grass to germinate.

A likely reason for this is improvement in soil health and the soil ecosystem. Cereal crops like oats and wheat exude sugars, or exudates, through their roots and into the soil. The sugars that are being secreted feed and stimulate soil microbes that are in turn creating a healthy environment around the rhizosphere of the plant. This healthy environment creates an ideal germination site for perennial seeds that are in the soil.

The obvious question is why doesn't this happen with crops that are zero- tilled? The answer most probably lies with the way zero till crops are grown when compared with Pasture Cropping. Pasture Cropping uses very low rates of herbicide or no herbicide at all, significantly reduced fertiliser, and no insecticide or fungicide when compared to zero-till cropping methods, which use substantial amounts of pesticides and fertiliser. The high rates of pesticide and fertiliser used with zero-till cropping methods kill soil microorganisms and destroy the soil ecosystem, which is required for the germination of perennial seeds.

The recruitment of perennial grass from existing seed in the soil by Pasture Cropping has been confirmed from many sources.

On Winona, the perennial grass has changed from 10% of

Winona in 1995 to 87% in 2010, and the number of species increased from 9 to over 50 in the same period.

Research work in 2006 and 2007 on the recruitment of native perennial grass was done by R. Thapa, , D. R. Kemp, D. L. Michalk, W. B. Badgery, and A. T. Simmons from Charles Sturt University in Orange, NSW.

A summary showed:

The pasture-cropped treatment had substantially higher seedling numbers than the un-grazed or the grazed treatment.

Where extra seed was added, and low-level herbicide applied had the highest initial recruitment of 279 seedlings per square metre and also had the highest number of young plants of 11 plants per square meter surviving.

A research project in 2009, run at the Land Institute on the outskirts of Salina in Kansas USA compared Pasture Cropping to zero-till cropping as a method of better managing land that has expired from the Conservation Reserve Program. Amongst many conclusions, they found Pasture Cropping stimulated an increase in perennial grass species, an increase in available nitrogen, increase in soil microbiology and increase in profit.

A pasture cropping sequence where a crop of oats has been sown into the dormant litter of warm-season C4 perennial grass. The crop yield was 3 ton/ ha

Outcomes

The development of Pasture Cropping and overlaying it with holistic grazing management has restored Winona's native grassland and changed my life.

Botanists have recorded over fifty species of native grassland plants on the property, the majority being grass species, but many are increasing numbers of forbs and herbs. This is a lot less than two hundred that Nicholas and Granny had in their grassland, but already the grassland species have changed Winona.

The continually regenerating grassland has improved the quantity and quality of stock feed. No longer does the property have an annual summer drought because most years the grass reaches almost to the top of the fences. In the winter period, sub clover that Harry planted in the 1950s is growing very happily amongst many native cool-season grass species. The combination of grassland plants with crops that are Pasture Cropped into them during winter has improved soil quality, soil structure, water infiltration, and soil carbon. Soil carbon has increased by over two hundred percent which has boosted water holding capacity and soil nutrients. The increase in soil nutrients has allowed me to eliminate the use of superphosphate, with none being applied since 1979, and crop fertiliser has been reduced by seventy percent. Even with a reduction in fertiliser, all the soil nutrients have increased by over one hundred and sixty percent.

Winona is now a functioning ecosystem that has attracted huge numbers of beneficial insects, spiders, and birds, which has eliminated the use of insecticides because crops and pasture are no longer attacked by insects. The restored soil ecosystem now has an abundant and diverse range of soil microbes which protect crops and pasture from disease, and are instrumental in increasing soil carbon.

Life has become far easier and much more profitable. Winona now produces a similar amount of wool as it did previously, but the quality is better and has a greater value. Because the feed quality is better the number of lambs that the property produces has increased. Grain yields from the crops are almost unchanged but are grown with over 80% less cost and the grazing value of areas before crop planting and after harvest has increased substantially.

The enterprises on Winona are now fully integrated which means that they all complement each other financially and ecologically. This allows for an improvement in overall production and creates substantial cost savings. These cost savings are enormous when compared to the previous industrial agriculture used on Winona. The integrated, self-supporting method of agriculture now creates an annual saving of over eighty thousand dollars and generates more income.

Pasture Cropping is being adopted around the world and is being acknowledged by farmers and scientists in many countries. USA scientist and crop researcher Dr Dwane Beck of Dakota Lakes Research Farm made these comments about Pasture Cropping.

Pasture Cropping has the best possibility of producing grain sustainably in Australia. I think the approach has tremendous potential.   (Dr Dwayne Beck 16th June 2014)

I did not realise it at the time, but I had developed a method of sowing crops that was unique. Ever since the first person planted crops in Mesopotamia 10,000 years ago humans have grown crops by killing everything except the planted crop. By mimicking Mother Nature, it became possible to restore grassland, soil and ecosystems while also growing crops. This was perhaps the most significant thing since the Mesopotamians developed agriculture. Agriculture did not have to destroy farmland and ecosystems while growing crops. Agriculture could restore both.

❧ 5 ❧

GRAZING MANAGEMENT

Sheep are believed to be the first herbivores to be domesticated in the Fertile Crescent of Western Iran, Turkey Syria and Iraq over 10,000 years ago when the people realised that it was easier to tame sheep and goats than chase them with a spear. It is thought that hunters might have brought orphaned animals back to their homes and kept them long enough to reach maturity and begin breeding. Sheep were not merely bred for meat, but to also provide milk, hide for leather, and later wool. Over thousands of years, humans experimented with the domestication of many species. But only a few like the cow, goat, sheep, chicken, horse, pig, dog and cat have proved themselves so useful that humans have distributed them all over the world.

Cattle are most likely the most important domesticated animal in the history of humanity, providing meat, dairy products, leather, manure for fertiliser, and later trained to pull a plough. It has now been revealed ancient people nearly didn't succeed in domesticating cattle at all. The reason for this is that the wild ancestors of cows, known as aurochs, were almost too wild to tame. The aurochs, or the wild ox (*Bos primigenius*), which has been extinct since 1627, was once common throughout Europe, northern Africa, and southern Asia and are believed to have been domesticated in south-east Turkey about nine to ten thousand years ago. It has now been shown that either most domestication attempts failed or most people simply thought trying to tame these wild, unpredictable creatures too difficult to even attempt. However, the ancient people who persisted with this volatile feral beast for a thousand years finally saw it become the domesticated cow we know today.

Humans had been hunter-gatherers for over 200,000 years, and around 10,000 years ago changed to a lifestyle of cultivating the soil and herding animals. This transformation is one of the most significant changes in human history and marks the dawn of the modern era, which had enormous ecological and human consequences.

Grazing animals are often regarded as being detrimental to the landscape, but for millions of years large wild herds of grass-eating herbivores migrated over vast areas, being pushed along by predators over the grasslands. These herds grazed, manured, and mulched the soil as they moved around the grassland and have been instrumental in creating and maintaining grasslands around the world by fertilising, creating topsoil and deepening plant roots. Without animals, there would not have been vast grasslands in most continents of the world.

During the time of domestication of animals, the wild herds were replaced by small numbers of domesticated, managed livestock which were contained in smaller areas for ease of control. It is the management of domesticated animals over many thousands of years that have created significant damage to grasslands, landscape and soil in almost all continents of the world. Why did wild animals create grasslands, and domesticated animals destroy it? The answer is obvious: humans have done a terrible job managing grazing animals for thousands of years. When animals were contained in one area, it prevented the constant forward movement of a vast number of animals. The animals stayed much longer in one area, and plant species were killed by the animals continually eating and not allowing them to regrow. This stopped the cycle of biological decomposition, and the once fertile, carbon-rich soils turned into dry, bare, arid land. It is not animals that are the problem, but the way they are managed by humans, and this is the main reason why grassland and soil have been destroyed.

In less than 200 years significant damage has been inflicted on Australia's grasslands and soil after Europeans introduced sheep and cattle. The loss of Australia's grasslands also caused severe loss of soil, and soil carbon, with carbon levels now measuring less than half of what the soil contained in the 1840s.

There is an urgency to manage the world's grazing animals better, so that grasslands, soil, and ecosystems can be restored. Some people have been aware of this human problem and have developed improved methods of grazing management. One of the very early pioneers of rotational grazing in the 1950s was the French scientist / farmer Andre Voisin. Andre Voisin was a French biochemist by training, but a farmer by preference. He was a great observer, and he researched pasture and grazing management by watching his cows graze his fields near Normandy, in France.

Over sixty years ago he established that overgrazing was a function of how long a plant was exposed to grazing and how long it was before it was re-grazed, which inspired his "rational grazing" management plan theory.

Below is a quote from Andre Voisin's book, first published in 1959

"Before a sward, sheared with the animal's teeth, can achieve its maximum productivity, sufficient interval must have elapsed between two successive shearings to allow the grass:

(a) to accumulate in its roots the reserves necessary for a vigorous spurt of re-growth;

(b) to produce its 'blaze of growth' (or high daily yield per acre)."

"The rest period between two successive shearings varies with the season, climatic conditions and other environmental factors."

The idea of holistic planned grazing began in the 1960s when Allan Savory, who was then a young wildlife biologist in his native Southern Rhodesia. The following excerpt has been supplied by Allan Savory:

During his time as a wildlife biologist in the grasslands of Africa, Allan Savory observed the movements of large herds of game. He noted that when pack-hunting predators were present animals bunched together for safety and that this behavior had a dramatic effect on the ground: their hooves broke up the soil, trampled old, grey stems and leaves to the ground where they could start to decay, and scattered seeds and covered them over with soil, dung and urine. Savory concluded that in these grassland environments, relatively high numbers of large, herding animals concentrated and moving as they naturally do when pack-hunting predators are present, are vital to maintaining the health of grasslands. Humans broke this connection, he believed, when they domesticated wild grazers and removed their predators. Herds relaxed and spread out; un-bunched, the animal hooves no longer trampled down plants or chipped and aerated soil surfaces. Land health and productivity began to decline, often rapidly.

Savory also reasoned that animals that bunch closely to ward off predators also dung and urinate in high concentration and thus foul the ground and plants on which they are feeding. No animals normally like to feed on their own faeces. Thus, to be able to feed on fresh plants the once vast game herds had to keep moving off the areas they had fouled. And they could not, ideally, return to the fouled area until the dung and urine had weathered and worn off.

This meant that plants and soils would have been exposed to massive disturbance in the form of grazing, trampling, dunging and urinating, but only for a day or so, followed by a period of time which gave the soil and plants an opportunity to recover. The same rules would apply in the case of livestock, which Savory began to work with in the 1960s, when ranchers, intrigued by his ideas, sought his help. The need to manage the length of time plants and soils were exposed and re-exposed to grazing animals led Savory to develop a grazing planning procedure that enabled ranchers to use concentrated livestock, constantly moving, to provide the same benefits to plants and soils once provided by wild herds.

Holistic Planned Grazing enables any farmer, rancher, or pastoralist to produce the best possible plan at any time by adding value to the knowledge he or she invariably has already in his or her head. It is an extremely effective way of addressing the full complexity involved when managing soil, plants, animals, and integrating the animals with any other activities on that land.

Most people cannot deal with more than a few variables at once and none can plan the complexity involved in managing livestock to regenerate grasslands and livelihoods using only their memory, a notebook, or calendar. So, the planning is done by following a series of simple steps in a specific order and recording the results on a grazing chart that gradually reveals where the herd should and should not be at certain times. Herd moves are then plotted, to ensure that animals are where they need to be at the right time, and with the right behavior (based on what one is trying to achieve).

Holistic Planned Grazing has been used for nearly fifty years in a variety of situations—from the margins of true deserts with almost no rainfall to tropical forests with abundant rainfall. The secret to its success is nothing more than trusting the procedure, following it, and recognizing that it, like all planning, is a continuous process—plan, monitor, control, and replan. - Allan Savory.

GRAZING ON WINONA

During the 1980s, I had heard of Allan Savory and how he had developed a method of grazing based on how the large wild herds of African animals grazed the African savanna. I did not fully comprehend Allan Savory's 'Holistic Planned Grazing' and could see many problems with this method of grazing, and thought it could not possibly work. The things I saw wrong with this type of grazing management approach was the extra work in moving sheep more often, the more mature grass unable to fatten animals and the moving making it more difficult as well, and sheep preferring not to be in a large mob. These same reasons are still given today by people that do not understand, or do not want to understand, this different livestock management method.

In 1989, with no knowledge or experience in this type of grazing management, I put one thousand ewes in one mob, and moved them every few days around a 500-acre section of the property. Within three months I had proven myself wrong, and all of my preconceived ideas about planned grazing I now saw were incorrect. Even over this short period the grazing method worked so well I could see that the sheep, grass and ground cover were all improving, and I looked at how I could expand this type of grazing to all of Winona.

At that time there was a lot of criticism of Alan Savory's grazing methods by many people including Government agency staff and other experts. The one person who wasn't critical was my father, who said when asked: "Yes, that will work if you move the mob often." That comment summed up Harry perfectly – a man who had done things differently all of his life and was always seeking new and better ways of doing things. The criticism of Holistic Planned Grazing and Allan Savory's work is entirely unjustified, and I am continually astounded by negative comments from many people including scientists who should look at the technique with a more open mind. I was to experience a similar adverse reaction a few years later as I started to develop Pasture Cropping.

In the early 1990s, I began to look at how I could further improve the grazing management on Winona using Holistic Planned Grazing.

The legacies of high fertiliser use and introduced pasture from the 1950s were weeds and bare ground. If I concentrated on increasing ground cover, I thought, the weeds would fix themselves. Gardens have been managed for many hundreds if not thousands of years by applying mulch to control weeds and conserve water so why wouldn't litter from the grassland do the same on Winona?

With my primary focus on creating litter and some fundamental knowledge of Allan Savory's grazing techniques, I decided to run as few mobs as possible to simplify the grazing management, and create long plant recovery time. The property had most of the internal fences re-built after the fire in 1979, and we had about 15 smaller paddocks of around 12 – 15 hectares for stud mating and lambing. The other paddocks were larger with areas of approximately 40 – 60 hectares (100-150 acres).

Creating large mobs seems like a simple task of putting all of the sheep together, but for the last 200 years in Australia, or at least since fences were built, sheep were run in smaller mobs that were related to age and sex. The ewes would be kept away from wethers, and each age group would also be separated. I could never see why this was done except for tradition, and that was the way everyone's grandfather did it, so it must be the correct way to graze animals.

Over recent years I have been asked about running wethers and ewes together, and problems at mating time. My usual answer is that the rams know the difference between a ewe and wether. Up until now, I was running mobs of around three hundred sheep, separated into age groups. The sheep were moved to a new, ungrazed paddock when the area was thoroughly grazed or the sheep had started to lose weight. The time on each paddock was usually around 3-4 weeks. This was the way Harry had very successfully managed his sheep for the last 60 years, and it was the way Nicholas and Granny ran their sheep over 100 years previously. The grazing methods that every generation of the family used since the 1870s was very successful; it was their management that enabled me to own Winona now. Should I change something that had been so successful? This concerned me for some time until I started recollecting the stories passed down to my father by Granny, about the paddocks covered with kangaroo grass and swaying in the breeze like a crop of oats. I looked at what I had in front of me now. The grassland had been replaced with weeds and bare ground with only a few kangaroo grass stalks on one tiny section of Winona. I had no choice; I would be irresponsible if I did not try to fix Winona by restoring the grassland.

I decided to run three sheep mobs, one with one thousand hoggets on ten paddocks and the other with two thousand five hundred adult ewes and wethers on twenty-five paddocks. The rams were run separately in a small group on five paddocks. This method worked well and allowed around three to four months for grass recovery after the sheep had grazed the area.

But as with anything new, there were unforeseen problems.

Sheep rushing through gate openings don't seem much of a problem, and it is something that sheep often do. But it becomes a problem when there are two thousand sheep involved. One day when I was moving a large mob through a gate opening into the adjoining paddock when one sheep stumbled and the following two thousand sheep tripped and fell. Suddenly I had a pile of sheep that could not be seen over and the ones on the bottom of the pile were dying of suffocation. After untangling the mess of legs and wool and removing about twenty dead sheep, I thought that I should find a better way of moving the large mob through a gateway. The answer was obvious; do not allow the sheep to rush through the gate. The easy way to achieve this was to stand at the gateway and allow my dog to bring the sheep to me, which put me in a position to control and slow down their movement. My son Nicholas has taken this a step further. If his sheep rush into a paddock he re-musters them and settles the sheep before allowing them to move slowly into the new area. These methods of calming the sheep have changed their behaviour and they now rarely rush through a gateway, and have become much easier to manage.

I found the larger paddocks of over forty hectares (100 acres) were not well grazed by the sheep, and the smaller paddocks were being grazed more evenly. Over time the larger paddocks were subdivided, and now Winona has seventy-five paddocks with most of them around twelve hectares (about 30 acres) in size. Each paddock has a water supply, with a small dam in each.

Another problem that I encountered was when the ewes were lambing (giving birth to their lambs). This is usually over six weeks, and it is less stressful on the ewes and lambs if the mobs are not moved often, but this can be a challenge for people that have large mobs of animals. I started to trial lambing the main group of 2000 merino ewes in one large mob, but I was not happy with some ewes losing their lambs so I split them into lambing groups of 300-400 ewes, which are slowly rotated around four to five paddocks. The stud ewes are mated and lambs born in small mobs of fifty ewes. Once the lambs are earmarked, and tails removed, all of the ewes and lambs are put together in one large mob of over four thousand including lambs, and rotated around the whole property.

Having them in one mob has the advantage of the ewes teaching the lambs about moving into new paddocks, but more importantly, the ewes teach their lambs which plants are suitable to eat.

. . .

COLIN SEIS

Grazing Plants

There are many advantages of grazing management methods that allow plants to recover before they are re-grazed, but some of the more important are, restoration of grasslands, the creation of soil surface litter, improvement of soil health and soil hydrology, and reduction of weeds.

Farms that are managed with continuous grazing methods, where animals are left in the same area for extended periods, are often dominated by less desirable and unpalatable plant species and the soil is lacking soil structure, with poor nutrient cycling, and declining soil carbon. Some of the reason for this deterioration in grassland and soil ecology is that grass plants have a fibrous root system that is often described as a mirror image of the leaves of the plant, meaning that leaves and roots have approximately the same biomass. During the grazing process, removal of the leaves by animals results in roots being pruned, or reduced to roughly match the area of the leaves. In other words, short leaves produce short roots. Continuous uncontrolled grazing of the most palatable plant species in grassland causes constant root pruning which reduces root biomass and creates plants with short and small root systems.

Livestock will continually select the most palatable plant species. If these plants are overgrazed with continuous grazing, both the leaf area and roots are kept short. Having small roots prevents them from competing effectively with the less palatable, un-grazed weedy species which, because they are not grazed, will have deeper and more vigorous roots. Having a larger root system gives the un-grazed weedy plants the advantage of being able to obtain more water and nutrients, while the more palatable plants are unable to source enough water and nutrients and the often die as a result. The less palatable species, meanwhile, mature, set seed and eventually dominate the pasture or grassland.

If the area is continued to be grazed without rest, the

remaining species will also be eaten short, and the roots will also be short. The short root system and lack of plant biomass will have severe effects on the hydrology of the area, creating plant water shortages, poor soil structure, ineffective nutrient cycling, and eventual loss of plants and a collapse of the soil ecosystem, and ultimately the farm.

The effect grazing has on plants has been known for a long time, but unfortunately very few people recognised the importance of the work that Franklin. J. Crider did in 1954. Crider worked with the United States Department of agriculture conducting several experiments using various perennial grasses, evaluating the effects that forage removal has on root growth.

"His work showed that a single graze, which removed most of the foliage, caused root growth to stop for up to eighteen days. Stoppage usually occurred within twenty-four hours and continued until recovery of the top of the plant was well advanced. When grazing was repeated periodically, as happens with continuous grazing, all of the grasses root growth stopped for periods that ranged from twenty-five to forty-five days. When the plants were more severely grazed with ninety percent, removal of the leaf area, three times per week, the effects on the roots were far more brutal. This severe grazing stopped root growth of one hundred percent of the plants which did not recover while ever the plant was grazed short during the duration of the experiment.

The conclusion of the research by Crider emphasised that the growing top of a grass plant cannot be reduced by more than half without adversely affecting the functioning of the root system and the plant as a whole. The complete stoppage of root growth is of particular significance because the continuous suppression of above ground growth and the inability of the plant to replenish food reserves have lasting effects on root inactivity. Thus weakened, the plant is less able to resist grazing, erosion, drought, cold, and disease" -Franklin. J. Crider

. . .

ONE MAY WONDER WHY THIS SIGNIFICANT WORK WAS NOT listened to, but this was the mid-1950s, and the 'green revolution' was in full swing. The answers lay in more fertiliser and pesticides and breeding better, more productive plants, not managing what we have with better grazing techniques.

A better grazing method that allows plants to recover before re-grazing permits the plants to grow large with an extensive root system. If those large plants are grazed in a single short event, it will stimulate a significant proportion of roots to die within a few hours of the removal of the leaves, to equalise the biomass of the removed leaves. As this happens the pruned roots supply valuable organic matter to the soil, which improves the soil's physical, chemical and biological quality.

The grazing process needs to be carefully managed, by using intermittent grazing and resting to invigorate the growth of new leaves and to provide pruned roots as organic matter for soil biota. This grazing process also creates dense soil surface litter which prevents weeds from germinating, restricts evaporation of water from the surface of the soil and maintains more constant soil temperature.

This type of grazing management, which allows plants to fully recover after a grazing event, can be used to restore farms and ecosystems by stimulating areas to transition from annual weeds to perennial plants, and then on to diverse grassland.

❧ 6 ❧

GRASSLANDS

The earth's rainforests are often called the "lungs of the planet" because they draw in carbon dioxide and breathe out oxygen. If rainforests are regarded as the lungs of the planet then the original grasslands could be called the heart of the planet, because 10,000 years ago grasslands covered over 40% of the earth's land area and were one of the most important ecosystems on the planet. Grasslands contributed significantly to maintaining climate, creating soil, providing wildlife habitat, water storage, and watershed protection for major river systems and supplying food many of the world's wild animals and humans. Much of the food that is grown as annual crops such as wheat, oats, barley, corn and sorghum, to name a few, were selected originally from the world's grasslands.

The planet's rainforests have received much attention in recent years because they are being decimated by the pursuit of agriculture, which is causing massive environmental and ecological damage. The planet's grassland destruction and the associated environmental loss this has created seems to have been overlooked. Grasslands are amongst the most endangered ecosystems on earth.

The annihilation of the world's grasslands started with the advent of agriculture 10,000 years ago, and since that time they have been systematically destroyed and replaced with annual crops and bare eroding soil. The grasslands have been destroyed because the fertile soil they created over millions of years was ideal for grazing domesticated animals and growing crops like wheat and corn, which are used to feed the growing human population. The ecological and environmental damage done by poorly managed domestic animals and ploughing grasslands to grow annual crops is rarely considered. Many of the planet's problems, such as degraded soil, increasing greenhouse gas, changing climate, silted rivers and polluted water, are directly related to the destruction of the world's grasslands.

Photosynthesis is the most important biological process on Earth. It is the primary source of almost all life, and the basis of all agriculture production.It is the process that plants use to capture energy from the sun and convert carbon dioxide from the air and water from the soil into carbohydrates, which are used to fuel the plant's growth. Throughout this process, oxygen is released from the plant as a waste product, which is critical for maintaining atmospheric oxygen levels and supporting life on Earth.

Over many millions of years, plants have evolved and modified the photosynthetic process to adapt to different climatic conditions.

The most common form of photosynthesis is called C3 photosynthesis. The majority of the plants on the planet are cool season C3 species that have evolved over hundreds of millions of years to be tolerant of cool wet conditions and grow well at temperatures within a range of 15 to 25 degrees Celsius. However, these plants are not tolerant of hot conditions and become less active or dormant as temperatures and light intensity increase and do not grow well at temperatures over 25 degrees Celsius.

Wheat, rice, oats and barley are annual examples of C3 plants. A more recent evolutionary innovation in plants happened about 30 million years ago when grasses developed a more efficient form of this process is called C4 photosynthesis, which is believed to be an adaption to hot and dry environments. This means that C4 plants can sustain higher rates of photosynthesis and produce more carbohydrate than C3 plants in hot, dry conditions. This gives them a competitive advantage over plants which rely on the more common C3 photosynthesis under conditions of drought, high temperatures, and carbon dioxide limitation. Most C4 plants function best within a temperature range of 25 to 35 degrees Celsius but are intolerant of low temperatures and go into dormancy at temperatures of below 15 degrees Celsius.

There are estimated to be 391,000 species of plants on the planet of which only 3% are C4 species

Examples of C4 annual plants include corn, sorghum, sugarcane and millet.

Australia's Grasslands
Australia was once part of the southern supercontinent,

Gondwana, which existed from approximately 570 million years ago and included most of the continents, in the present day, Southern Hemisphere, including Antarctica, South America, Africa, Madagascar, India and Australia. Around 50 million years ago Australia severed its last links with Gondwana as it separated from Antarctica.

The evidence of Gondwana still exists today with similar plants in many Gondwanan countries. The *Proteaceae* family of plants, which include the Waratah, Protea and Banksia, grow only in southern South America, South Africa and Australia, are considered to have a "Gondwanan distribution". Most modern Australian flora had their origin 145 – 65 million years ago in Gondwana during the Cretaceous period when Australia was covered in subtropical rainforest. Australian ferns and gymnosperm today display a strong resemblance to their Gondwanan ancestors. Many early Gondwanan angiosperm flora or flowering plants such as the Nothofagus, Myrtaceae and Proteaceae were also present in Australia. There are many of the same grassland species in Australia, Africa and India and it is thought that these species have Gondwanan connections.

The first plants emerged from a watery environment and started growing on land around 450 million years ago during the Ordovician period. Plants continued to evolve until grass species made their appearance around 50-60million year ago. It is thought that most of the early plants had a C3 photosynthetic pathway, and C4 plants evolved much later. In Australia, there is evidence to suggest that C4 grass species evolved around 30 million years ago during the Oligocene period. The C4 pathway originated when grasses migrated from the shady forest canopy to more open areas where high sunlight gave it an advantage over the C3 pathway. Carbon dioxide levels dropped, and the climate became hotter and drier around 6 to 7 million years ago, during the Miocene period. During this time the C4 grass species thrived and the diverse Australian grassland as we know it today was born.

Australia's grassland was different from many grasslands globally because it was dominated by warm season (C4) perennial species that had evolved to grow in hot and dry environments at the time of European settlement. Over 1100 native grass species grow in Australia, of which most are warm-season (C4) with only a small proportion of cool-season (C3) perennial species. The dominance of warm-season C4 grass species indicates that Australia's climate has been hot and dry for an extremely long period.

The growth pattern and co-existence of the two grass types is remarkable because these grassland plants utilise resources separately. In the hotter months, warm-season C4 grass grows profusely, while cool-season C3 grass becomes dormant to avoid the hot and dry climate. During Australia's winter months, the warm season C4 grass becomes dormant to avoid the cold temperatures, and the cool season C3 grass grows. It was this growth pattern and natural dormancy that enabled the development of 'pasture cropping.'

These two grass species grow amongst each other supplying protection from the elements, complementing each other, supplying food for, and encouraging microorganisms that live in the soil among their roots. In species diverse grassland as existed pre-European settlement, there were always plants growing at any one time. Between the grass tussocks grew a vast diversity of flowering forbs and herbs such as orchids, lilies, iris and geraniums, and climbing over the tussocks were leguminous pea-like plants such as glycine and desmodium which are perennial herbs.

In 1788, when the first fleet arrived in Australia with its cargo of 1373 convicts, marines and seamen much of Australia was covered in grassland with scattered trees. The open 'park-like' grasslands were not an accident of nature but were created by careful and skilful fire management by the

Australian Indigenous people who had manipulated the grassland and Australia's ecosystems for 2000 generations. Over tens of thousands of years, Australia's native people learned how to manage the landscape to provide a reliable source of food. Despite the current view of hunting as the main food source, the grasslands were an essential source of their diet where perennial lilies and orchids and tubers from Murnong or Yam Daisy were staples, and seed from grass species was ground into flour.

In the 1820s when my great great, great, great, grandparents William and Eleanor Moore were granted their farm west of Sydney, the area was described as park-like with grass and scattered trees, but it changed very quickly when Indigenous land management was stopped. Less than thirty years later in 1848, explorer Thomas Mitchell described the area near Sydney as:

'Where a man might gallop without impediment and see whole miles before him, the omission of the annual periodical burning by natives of the grass and young saplings has already produced in the open forest lands nearest to Sydney, thick forests of young trees... Kangaroos are no longer to be seen there, the grass is choked by underwood; neither are there natives to burn the grass nor is fire longer desirable among the fences of the settlers.' (Mitchell, 1848)

In 1818 John Oxley was exploring the country along the Macquarie Rivernear where the city of Dubbo now stands, one hour drive west of my property Winona. His written comments were: *'Many hills and elevated flats were entirely clear of timber, and the whole had a very picturesque and park-like appearance.'*

The openness of trees and quality and quantity of the grassland is written about often during the first eighty to ninety years of settlement in Australia. When Nicholas Seis first selected his small farm in 1868, the tree density was described as 'open forest' meaning it would indeed have had a park-like appearance.

Grasslands have been lost over most of our planet, and South Eastern Australia is no different. There are very few C4 native grass species left in much of the states of Victoria, Southern New South Wales, and South Australia. This lack of species has stimulated a debate saying that C4 grass species will not grow in those areas. Much of Southern Australia has a Mediterranean climate where the rainfall is predominantly in winter with less summer rain. But the true reason that there are few C4 native grass species in these areas is not lack of summer rainfall, but because the farming and grazing methods used since European settlement in the 1840s have killed much of the grassland species and replaced them with introduced species and weeds. The species change altered much of the grassland ecosystem which created significant hydrology problems such as waterlogging in wet seasons and hard compacted soil in dry seasons.

Much of southern Australia experiences an annual summer drought. Not because it doesn't rain in the summer, but because the C4 grass species have been removed and now there are very few summer grass species left. The removal of warm-season C4 species has created another insidious dilemma. The introduced cool-season species are dormant and dry during the hot summer months, which creates a severe fire hazard and a significant reason why bush-fires are common and fierce in these areas of Australia.

The problems of summer droughts, salinity and waterlogging are continuing because the grassland that controlled the hydrology, soil and soil structure is now gone, lost in much the same way that it had been destroyed at Winona. The magnitude of the loss of grassland has not been comprehended because the grassland had been replaced with supposedly better, more productive cool-season C3 species and few people realise the significance of the loss of the ecosystem because of the destruction of the grassland species diversity. The answer is to re-establish the function of the grassland and restore it closer to how George Augustus Robinson saw it in 1841. This can be done with native species, but it can also be achieved with a diverse range of introduced C3 and C4 perennial species which function as the original grassland did for millennia.

In 1839 George Augustus Robinson was appointed Chief Protector of Aborigines for Port Phillip (Victoria) and travelled extensively throughout the region as he had done in Van Diemen's Land (Tasmania). He was one of the first to describe life outside the early colonial settlements. While travelling through the western district in 1841, his daily journal recounts Victorian landholders' lives and times in the mid-1800s. His journal also contains fascinating insights into the local Indigenous culture - and an extraordinarily account of the landscape he travelled through while undertaking his work.

Robinson's journal makes many references to 'green grass' - even in the height of summer, when the daily temperatures were often above 37 degrees Celsius. An important point to emerge from the colonial records is that warm season C4 species dominated the summer-green, perennial grasslands which greeted early settlers.

This is an extract from his diary, edited by Gary Presland and published as part of the Records of the Victorian Archaeological Survey (Presland 1977).

Friday 10 January 1840 "The country through which we travelled today consisted of green hills and valleys with a verdure of transparent green. The sun was hot and the bright green of the grass, contrasted with the sombre foliage of the trees, had a delightful appearance. The roads and soil were good, and the country on either side of the road as far as the eye could scan was truly luxuriant."

Friday 24 January 1840 "Followed round by the creek about a mile beyond Mt Campbell on the west side, returned a mile and then crossed the creek opposite the mount and rode over some stony hills, and ascended the mount. The day was fine and view clear. Rode half way up, then tethered our horses and walked to the summit. To the N. and N.W. as far as the eye could scan was a boundless plain and an ocean like appearance. Due N., distant about 10 miles from Mt Campbell, observed extensive grassy plains extending in the direction of the Goulburn River. Mr Hutton has been on the plains and represents the soil to be a deep rich mould. He thrust [a] stick two feet into the soil and it was of [the] same description, and yet deeper. …The country to the S. and west good grassy country, undulating and extending as far as the eye could reach. (Note: Mt Campbell is today known as Mt Camel).

There are references throughout Robinson's journal in the height of summer to grassy valleys and plains, luxuriant, verdant meadows, carpets of colourful flowers and creepers, and Indigenous women with 'large heaps of murnong' (yam daisy tubers).

Many of the rivers were described as rush-lined chains of ponds which contained abundant

large fish, eels, and crayfish.

There are also references to patches of trees and forests in Robinson's journal, but it is evident that the early settlers in the medium to low rainfall areas of Victoria did not need to clear trees for their sheep and cattle runs or their small-scale cropping (wheat, barley and vegetables). The woody vegetation referred to by Robinson was principally native cherry

(*Exocarpus*), honeysuckle (*Banksia*) and oak (*Casuarina*) and

many of the hills were described as treeless or with only
scattered trees.

The description and references by Robinson were very
typical of grasslands around Australia at that time. Still,
regrettably, the early settlers did not realise that the landscape
and grassland was a manmade and nurtured environment.
Without the knowledge passed down by the original
Indigenous custodians, the grassland and ecosystem were
destined to collapse.

As the grassland and ecosystems around Australia
declined with European land management and overgrazing
by introduced sheep and cattle, attempts were made to
maintain production by adding pasture species from the
northern hemisphere. The introduction of new species was
intended to improve the degraded grassland and in some
cases create a European appearance by changing the plant
species that nature had taken millennia to perfect. Not
surprisingly many of the introduced grass species did not
perform well and either died or became weeds until the soil
chemistry was altered after the discovery and use of chemical
fertilisers in the 1920s. Phosphate fertiliser stimulated the
phosphorus dependant, introduced grasses to a point where
they became as productive as the grasses that evolved in
Australia aeons ago.

Wheat had been grown in eastern Australia from the early
1800s but it was not until the first quarter of the 20th century
that wheat-growing began in earnest. From the beginning of
the 1920s to the 1940s, tens of thousands of acres of native
grassland were destroyed with ploughs which were used to
prepare the soil to grow wheat and feed Australia's growing
nation,

It took in, human terms, decades before the consequences
of overgrazing, ploughing and the introduction of foreign
plants started to take effect, but in ecological terms, it was
instantaneous and catastrophic. Inappropriate grazing

management and the introduction of annual pasture plants and disc ploughs changed the water and nutrient cycles with dramatic results because the vast grasslands no longer existed to be able to control excess water. With the grasslands gone, much of the topsoil was lost together with its precious organic matter. The soils declined to such a degree that it created significant problems such as salinity, acid soils and severe soil erosion in the period from the 1920s onward. The eroding soil was deposited into the once pristine, clean rivers, filling them with silt from which they have never recovered.

We have not learned from our mistakes. Today much of Australia is still being poorly managed with livestock, and the methods used to grow crops are continuing to destroy grasslands which create bare soil and continue to fill Australia's rivers with silt.

Most Australian grasslands are now a shadow of their former selves, having only a few native species and dominated by introduced weeds. In Australia, we have decimated much of the grassland and associated ecosystems in less than 200 years. Many of the world's grasslands have had thousands of years of similar abuse with inappropriate land management. Much of the world's grazing and farming soils have become biological deserts that are propped up by expensive soil additives and fertilisers. These deserts have been produced primarily because of the absence of perennial plants, litter and ground cover, which are necessary to maintain the myriad of micro and macro soil organisms essential for the growth of healthy grasslands.

The loss of grasslands species which were replaced with plants that were never intended to grow in Australia has done considerable ecological damage. The sad part is that many people, including agricultural advisers, do not realise that replacement of plant species without considering the ecology of the landscape is doomed to fail. If a pasture requires re-sowing, it should function as the original grassland functioned, with a diverse range of species ranging from cool season C3 perennial grass, warm season C4 perennial grass, and forbs and herbs that mimic the original grassland. A diverse mix of species, functioning as grassland does many things. It supplies a food supply of litter and root exudates for the diverse range of soil microorganisms. The microbes supply and cycle nutrients to the plants and are crucial for increasing soil organic carbon. These same soil bugs are also essential for controlling plant diseases. The diverse grassland is also a host to a myriad of insects and spiders that keep plant-damaging insects under control and supply food to a diverse range of birds and reptiles.

Native grassland, with its abundant species diversity and balanced ecosystem, can be of great financial benefit. It is known that grasslands produce excellent feed for livestock, but grassland soil has a diverse range of soil microorganisms which are vital for cycling nutrients and increasing soil carbon. This can supply massive amounts of nutrients that can save thousands of dollars in fertiliser expenses.

Soil microorganisms also reduce the need to use fungicides by controlling soil-borne plant fungal disease. Grasslands also attract a large and assorted range of insects that play a vital role in maintaining a balance of insect species and preventing damaging insect attacks in pasture and crops, eliminating the need for insecticide.

All of these benefits are not only free but can be a massive saving in fertiliser, fungicide and insecticide purchases.

ॐ 7 ॐ

SOIL

'Globally, soils are chronically unhealthy. Nationally, overused chemical inputs and miss-placed farm programs continue to mask chronic symptoms of dis-functional soils. Billions of acres of uncovered-carbon depleted soils have impacted all biotic, climatic, and aquatic health. Eroded soil nutrients reach our water bodies but not our nutrient deficient human bodies. Why? We do not value our soils! We do not value what we do not understand! A majority of agricultural producers, technical personnel, and a majority of academia do not understand that soils are living ecosystems. How much less the general public. The current national soil paradigm-soil is dirt; a chemistry set and a growing medium that we force and control for efficiency. Soil is not dirt; it's alive! '
    Ray Archuleta

Ray Archuleta is a Certified Professional Soil Scientist with the Soil Science Society of America and has over 30 years experience as a Soil Conservationist, Water Quality Specialist, and Conservation Agronomist with the Natural Resources Conservation Service (NRCS). After his retirement from the NRCS in 2017, Ray founded

Understanding Ag, LLC, and Soil Health Academy, LLC, to teach Biomimicry strategies and Agroecology principles for improving soil function on a national scale. Ray also owns and operates a 150-acre farm near Seymour, Missouri that he operates along with his wife and family.

Most farm kids learn to drive at a very young age, and it has been this way before the internal combustion engine was invented and cars were even thought of. Children were taught to ride horses as soon as they could sit upright in the saddle and this same attitude spilt over to cars and tractors when they became available. The Seis family were no different and like most farm kids I, like my brothers and sister, was driving around the farm at five or six years old.

A problem with a kid of five driving is not the inability to steer the car, but legs that are too short to reach the clutch, brake and accelerator pedals. This was usually mastered by climbing down under the steering wheel, depressing the clutch, and manoeuvring the gear lever into first gear. With the right foot on the accelerator, you let the clutch out, which sends the car into a frenzied series of kangaroo hops. This may seem rather basic driving, but when you are only three feet tall and sitting on the floor while the vehicle is careering down the paddock, there is some urgency to see where you are going. Having climbed back onto the seat and peering through the steering wheel, the tree coming at you at breakneck speed is narrowly avoided, and you settle in to steer the beast without any more near misses. Most city dwellers would be horrified by this life-threatening and terrifying experience, but we loved it, and at that age were well supervised by my father who directed the driving lessons, ensuring no damage was done. As we became more competent by nine or ten years old, and our legs had grown longer, we were driving around Winona by ourselves with little supervision.

Learning to drive the tractor was done in a similar manner, but at an older age of thirteen or fourteen. At that age it was enjoyable, and I looked for any excuse to drive. My father would go with me for one or two laps around the paddock, instructing me at what speed I should travel, and where the plough should track so as not to create any uneven ploughed ground.

As well as the thrill of driving a tractor at such a young age, a lasting memory is one of smell. There is no way to put into words the smell of soil. The sweet smell of freshly ploughed soil is one that poetry is written about, and one which most farm kids remember their whole lives. Now I realise the smell of newly ploughed soil is the smell of death. The lives being lost are dying soil microbes as their home is being torn apart by the plough.

I apologise to readers for destroying the romance of farmers tilling the soil.

When I was a teenager the initial ploughing was done when the soil was wet, and the subsequent cultivation was done after the weeds had germinated and the soil was often dry. This work on a tractor without a cabin was hot and thirsty, and by day's end, everything was covered with a thick layer of fine dust including my hair and eyes.

My enthusiasm for tractor driving diminished.

My other childhood learning experience was not to drive around the paddocks in the farm truck, but to walk, after 3-4 inches (75mm-100mm) of rain. After that amount of rain the usually rock hard soil would turn into soup, and many times the farm truck or tractor would be stuck and bogged to the axles. One such time I was moving a mob of three hundred sheep into an adjacent paddock, walking so not to bog the farm truck. The sheep started to mill in a circle, the whole area turned to a kind of fawn coloured toothpaste, and the entire mob became stuck up to their bellies. It took many hours of hard, dirty, muddy work to free them from their potential death trap.

There was a very good reason the farm truck and the sheep became bogged on Winona, and it was not solely related to excess rain. After decades of ploughing and loss of perennial grassland, the soil had lost its enormous root mass that helped maintain its structure and the soil had become unstable, being rock hard when dry and sloppy mud when wet. I, like many people, thought that this was a typical feature of granite soil but now that the Winona grassland is restored, the soil and its structure has significantly improved, and is now able to absorb much more rain without becoming boggy.

My great grandfather Nicholas grew wheat crops into very soft friable soil that was created by the grassland over millennia. The ground was so soft that he was able to dig it with a hoe. My grandfather also grew excellent crops on that same land, but this time preparing the soil with a plough pulled by a horse team. With the use of a tractor in the early 1930s my father's wheat crops were almost six feet tall, but eventually the height of the crop and grain yield diminished as more soil was ploughed and wheat sown. During the Green Revolution years on Winona, wheat crops were propped up with chemical fertiliser and pesticides as the soil became more depleted in structure, carbon and life.

By the time the fire hit Winona in December 1979, the property had become degraded and dependent on high fertiliser inputs. The granite soil had become compacted, lacking structure, acidic, high in aluminium, and organic carbon levels had dropped from five percent levels of pre-European times to around one percent in 1979. The topsoil had declined to less than 100 mm (4 inches) deep, and the subsoil had become sodic. The poorly structured soil allowed very little water to infiltrate, which when combined with low soil carbon, considerably reduced soil health, affected nutrient cycling, and plant available nutrients. This had a flow-on effect to grass species, pasture production and crop yields, which required the addition of more fertiliser to correct the nutrient deficiencies.

Chemical, physical and biological soil properties characterise soil quality. The chemical properties of soil are often associated with soil fertility such as available nitrogen, phosphorus, potassium and micronutrients such as copper and zinc.

The physical properties of soil are structural characteristics such as aggregate formation, soil tilth, and soil texture.

The biological properties of soil are essential for combining soil physical and chemical properties. For example, bacteria and fungi recycle carbon, nitrogen, phosphorus, and other nutrients, into the mineral forms that can be used by plants, and some types of fungi which transfer nutrients and water to plants.

When we are walking on the ground, we are actually walking on top of another world, one that is perhaps more complex than the one we live in. There are so many microorganisms in the soil that a spoonful of healthy soil contains over six billion microbes.

Soil is not dirt. It might look like dirt, but it is the most abundant ecosystem on Earth. It is not merely bits of crushed rock that hold plants in a vertical position, but a combination of rocky, ground-up parent material, the remains of dead plants, minerals, gases, liquids, and a myriad of organisms that together support plant life. The soil is a living symbiotic ecosystem which is alive with billions of bacteria, fungi, protozoa, nematodes and other microbes that provide nutrients for plants, absorbs and stores rainwater, and provide habitat for soil microbes. The interaction of all of these species helps create healthy nutrient rich soil.

When the soil is ploughed, as I did when a teenager, soil microorganisms are killed by the action of the plough turning the soil over and exposing them to sunlight and heat. The smell that we all regard as 'a pleasant sweet, earthy smell' is actually a bacteria called *Streptomyces*, a genus of actinobacteria which gives off a chemical compound called geosmin as they die. It is geosmin, created by billions of dying bacteria that we smell from the freshly ploughed soil. This gives an indication of the damage ploughing and tilling the soil does.

The death of microbes is only a part of the destruction. Ploughing also contributes to soil erosion, soil compaction, nutrient and soil carbon decline, which were the cause of many of my problems from the 1970s onward.

Microbes and creatures living in the soil are critical to the health and quality of the soil. They affect the structure and therefore erosion and water availability. Most importantly, microbes protect crops from pests and diseases and are crucial for decomposition and nutrient cycling. As a result, they influence plant growth and as a consequence, affect animal and human health.

Over many millions of years, the growth of plants and grasslands has been responsible for the creation of topsoil. There are many thousands of different soil types on planet earth, and most soil formation begins with the accumulation of geological parent material that has broken down through weathering and glaciation over millions of years, but it is not soil until organic matter from plants is added to it. In other words, plants and their associated soil microbes are the creators of soil. Plants do this by living, dying, and adding organic matter to the surface of the ground and beneath the surface in the rooting zone. Organic matter decomposes until the original substance turns into a dark-coloured matter called humus. As well as promoting good soil structure and retaining soil water, humus serves as a source of nutrients for plants. The myriad of organisms such as bacteria and fungi use organic matter as a source of nutrients. As microorganisms decompose organic material, they release nutrients into the soil in forms that plants can use. This soil biomass is an integral part of the healthy soil ecosystem that is essential for agricultural production, but the soil ecosystem can be quickly destroyed by cultivation, overuse of fertilisers, herbicides, pesticides and exposure to surface light and heat.

Many mutually beneficial relationships have developed between plants and soil microbes. Over ninety percent of plants on planet earth have evolved to function in a symbiotic relationship with fungi, but the most important of these is the association between mycorrhizal fungi and plants. Mycorrhizal fungi penetrate the cells of the plant root without harming the plant and from the plant root the fungi extends a network of microscopic threads called hyphae through the soil. These threads or fungal hyphae can be regarded as a highly efficient transfer system, like a pipeline, between the soil and the plant. This transfer system moves water and nutrients to the plant in exchange for root exudates or sugars produced by the plant as a product of photosynthesis. The process also helps plants locate and transport scarce nutrients (including water) from beyond the nutrient depletion zone and from crevices and rocks the roots can't access.

Mycorrhizal fungi can only obtain food (sugars) from their

host plant. If the host plant is killed, they also die. They are thought to have a lifespan of up to 15 days and are therefore reliant on continual replenishment of new hyphae from spores (propagules) in the soil. The spores are adversely affected by fertiliser, heavy lime application, pesticide use, ploughing, and tillage.

While the addition of fertiliser is considered to have a positive impact on plant productivity, fertilisers containing soluble phosphorus will significantly reduce mycorrhizal fungi colonisation. Modern agriculture has created a vicious cycle. In a stable soil ecosystem, the fungi that supply nutrients to plants are killed by the fertiliser that provides nutrients to plants. This means plants become more dependent upon the soluble fertiliser for food as the fungi die. These soluble nutrients need to be resupplied to maintain productivity – thus continuing the cycle of fertiliser application. As well as fertiliser application, treatments that kill off the plants in the soil such as herbicide, ploughing and burning have an adverse impact on mycorrhizae by removal of their food source and destruction of their hyphal network. Without food, the fungi will not survive in sufficient numbers, and consequently, it is slower to recover once a new crop or pasture is sown.

This knowledge has resolved the dilemma that my Harry encountered in the 1970s when he saw reduced plant growth and loss in production on fertilised paddocks. Harry thought the phosphorus fertiliser had stopped working because pasture was not responding to fertiliser application. The agronomy advice was to double the amount of fertiliser, but the soil was not lacking phosphorus; it contained very low levels of mycorrhizal fungi, which were killed by the high rates of phosphorus fertiliser. The way to address this issue is not by applying more fertiliser, but restoring the fungi.

Restoring a soil ecosystem where mycorrhizal fungi and other microbes have been damaged with ploughing, fertilisers and herbicides can often be done quickly and cheaply. In fact, if it is done cleverly, the resulting decrease in fertiliser input costs can result in improved profitability. Recovering mycorrhizae populations can be achieved through the application of simple principles that remove limitations to the fungi and provide suitable habitat and nutrition for it.

The problems of depleted soil microbial populations were addressed on Winona after the fire in 1979 by simply not being able to afford to purchase superphosphate. When phosphorus fertiliser was no longer applied, and ploughing ceased in the 1980s, the soil ecosystem, including mycorrhizal fungi, started to recover along with the grassland. This process was significantly amplified by the oat crops that were Pasture Cropped into the perennial grass. Root exudates or sugars from the oat plants that were secreted into the soil was a perfect food source for the fungi, and when combined with additional root exudates and soil health benefits from the perennial grass during the summer months the fungi and associated soil microbes flourished.

The importance of healthy microbial rich soil, and how finely balanced the soil ecosystem was, made me realise how much damage had been innocently inflicted on Winona's soil and ecosystem. The realisation that the sweet, earthy smell that arose from ploughed soil was one of destruction and death, plus the awareness that ploughing was also killing the essential soil fungi and damaging the soil ecosystem, exposed the damage we had done. I now know why massive amounts of fertiliser had to be continually applied and the reason why our crops were plagued with disease.

SOIL CARBON

It is impossible to talk about soil without mentioning soil carbon, and I believe one of the highest authorities on soil carbon is Dr Christine Jones, who supplied the following section.

Organic carbon is the basic building block for all life on - and in - the earth. We cannot live without it. Neither can our soils. Carbon (C) provides the structural basis for thousands of different compounds. It is so common; we take it for granted. We often take hydrogen (H) and oxygen (O) for granted too - but where would we be without H_2O - our precious, life-sustaining water? The significance of soil water is becoming more apparent as we lose soil carbon. The carbon content and moisture-holding capacity of soil go hand in hand.

Organic carbon begins and ends its journey as a gas, carbon dioxide (CO_2). Atmospheric carbon is an extremely valuable resource. When sequestered in topsoil as organic carbon, it brings with it a wealth of environmental, productivity and quality of life benefits. An understanding of the 'carbon cycle' and the role of carbon in soils, is essential to our understanding of life on earth.

In the miracle of photosynthesis, which takes place in the chloroplasts of green leaves, carbon dioxide (CO_2) from the air and water (H_2O) from the soil, are combined to capture light energy and store it in the form of a simple sugar - glucose ($C_6H_{12}O_6$). Through a myriad of chemical reactions, this glucose is transformed to a great diversity of other carbon compounds, including complex sugars, starches, proteins, cellulose, plant hormones, organic acids, waxes and oils - and in previous geological eras, our 'fossil fuels' coal, oil and gas. We have a great deal to thank green leaves for!

Dinosaurs
Liquorice Allsorts
The clothes we wear
Me and you
All are carbon atoms in various patterns
Amazing what carbon can do!

The reason there are so many carbon compounds is that carbon atoms can link together to form an incredible variety of short chains, long chains, branched chains and rings, to which other elements, such as hydrogen and oxygen, can join. The study of carbon compounds is called organic chemistry.

Some carbon compounds are complex, while others are very simple. Gases like methane and ethane, and liquids like petrol, belong to a family called hydrocarbons, that is, carbon combined with hydrogen. The gas, carbon dioxide (CO_2), is simply carbon and oxygen. When carbon joins with both hydrogen and oxygen, it forms fats and oils, as well as carbohydrates such as the sugars and starches found in grains, vegetables and fruit. Proteins are formed from carbon, hydrogen, oxygen and nitrogen and often include other elements such as sulphur and phosphorus.

Representatives of all groups of carbon compounds are found in soils. These compounds are essential to the creation of 'topsoil' from the structureless, lifeless 'mineral soil' produced by the weathering of rocks.

Sadly, around 50 - 80% of the organic carbon that was once in the topsoil has been lost to the atmosphere over the last 150 years or so, due to our failure to take care of the earth as a living thing.

By inference, degraded soils have the potential to store up to five (5) times more organic carbon in their surface layers than they currently hold, provided we change the way we manage the land.

A net gain of organic carbon in soils is win-win for plants, animals and people. A net gain of carbon in the atmosphere is lose-lose. Our role, as managers of the carbon cycle, is to ensure that as much carbon as possible is returned to soils and as little as possible goes into the air.

According to the Food and Agriculture Organization of the United Nations (FAO), one-third of the world's arable soils are moderately to highly degraded, due to erosion, salinisation, compaction, acidification and chemical pollution. The deterioration of the world's soil resource has significant implications for food production.

With a rapidly increasing human population, it is imperative we quickly learn how to restore the carbon content and productivity of agricultural soils.

The most beneficial form of organic carbon for soil is exudation from the roots of actively growing green plants. Carbon additions are governed by the volume of plant roots and their rate of growth. The more active plant roots there are, the more carbon is added. It's as simple as that.

The effectiveness of Pasture Cropping as a soil restoration technique can be attributed to the integration of perennial grasses and annual crops in both space and time. The ongoing carbon additions from the perennial component evolve into highly stable forms of soil carbon, while the short-term, high sugar forms of carbon exuded by the roots of annual crops stimulate microbial activity.

In environments with only one growing season per year, the use of multi-species covers and in-crop companions (eg clover with wheat, peas with canola, legumes with corn and so on) can rapidly improve soil health.

In this positive feedback loop, CO_2 respired by plant roots and soil microbes moves upwards through the topsoil and increases the concentration of CO_2 beneath the crop or pasture canopy, enhancing photosynthesis. CO_2 is a trace gas in the atmosphere and often limits plant growth. This limitation can be overcome if soils are carbon-rich. As money makes money - so carbon makes carbon - but only when the management is right.

Under many conventional crop and pasture management regimes, the stimulatory effects of plant root exudates are negated by bare fallows, cultivation, herbicides, high-analysis fertilisers, pesticides and fungicides. Over time, organic carbon levels in soils subjected to these kinds of agricultural practices fall to levels where the soil is essentially 'dead'.

> *We once farmed Fields of Eden,*
> *we grew our food with style*
> *It's time to stop, and look, and listen for a while*
> *Earth lying naked and barren*
> *Crying for help without words*
> *Calling so softly for carbon*
> *There is no time now to bargain*

Recent research shows the earth's major continents are 'dewatering' at an alarming rate - that is, more water is being lost through evaporation and run-off than is received through precipitation. This disruption to the water cycle is due to loss of soil function.

Regenerative land management techniques such as Pasture Cropping, particularly when used in combination with multi-species covers, companion crops and adaptive multi-paddock grazing regimes such as utilised by practitioners of Holistic Management, can restore carbon and life to soil, conferring multiple ecological and productivity benefits. On-farm benefits include improved nutrient cycling, enhanced soil water storage, soil structural stability and disease suppression. Off-farm benefits include markedly improved catchment/ watershed function and enhanced water quality.

While improved groundcover management is the key to increasing the carbon content of soil, products that support soil microbial diversity and abundance, including a wide range of composted animal and plant materials (and extracts thereof), fish, seaweed, vermiliquid and vermicast, green manures and mulches, amino acids and biodynamic preparations, can also improve soil function, especially when combined with regenerative land management regimes.

Increasing the carbon content of soil is one thing. Keeping it there is another. Like water and nitrogen, carbon is in a constant state of flux between the atmosphere and the soil. Carbon additions therefore need to be combined with land management practices that foster the conversion of relatively transient forms of organic carbon to more stable complexes within the soil.

Carbon sources and carbon sinks

In cropped or grazed land supporting green plants for only part of the year, more carbon will move to the atmosphere than is sequestered. The establishment of forests, (including 'carbon sink' forests) also results in net losses in soil carbon, due to the lack of groundcover under the trees.

In these situations, the soil is said to be a net source of carbon.

Alternatively, cropped or grazed paddocks managed regeneratively act as carbon sinks. This means that more carbon is sequestered than is lost, improving productivity and soil water-holding capacity.

Stable soil carbon

Organic carbon moves between various 'pools' in the soil, some of which are short lived while others may persist for thousands of years. Glomalin and humus are two of the relatively stable forms of soil carbon. Their creation and destruction are strongly influenced by land management.

Glomalin

The relatively recent discovery of glomalin has caused a complete re-examination of what makes up soil organic matter and how we measure it. Glomalin is an insoluble glycoprotein (a compound containing both protein and sugar). It also contains quite high levels of iron, which is thought to help protect plants from pathogens. Glomalin is produced by arbuscular mycorrhizal fungi growing in association with plant roots. It can persist for several decades and may account for one-third of the organic carbon in agricultural soils.

Most members of the grass family are excellent hosts for glomalin-producing mycorrhizal fungi. Under healthy grassland there can be up to 100 metres of microscopic fungi per gram of soil. Enhanced glomalin formation may therefore help explain the success of regenerative land management practices such as Pasture Cropping.

Inhibitory factors for mycorrhizal fungi and glomalin production include bare soil, intensive tillage, the use of high-analysis phosphorus fertilisers and the growing of monocultures of plants in the Brassica family, such as canola, mustard, radish or turnips. Brassicas are not inhibitory to mycorrhizal fungi if grown in mixed culture with host plants such as legumes and grasses.

Humus

There is nothing recent about the discovery of humus, which dates back to Roman times. Despite being the best known of the stable organic fractions in soils, humus has never been clearly defined or understood. Even today, many aspects of the formation, composition, structure and function of humus remain somewhat of a mystery.

One reason for our lack of knowledge is that humus is an integral component of the soil matrix and cannot be successfully isolated for scientific research. Synthetic humus or extracted humic compounds do NOT have the same properties as the humus found naturally within the soil.

There are many theories on the formation of humus, most of which suggest a microbial resynthesis and polymerisation of carbon compounds derived from photosynthesis. If soil conditions are conducive to biological activity, the rate of humification can exceed estimates based on the weight of organic materials grown or applied. This suggests that carbon derived from root exudates may be the factor of greatest importance, emphasising the need for living plant cover for as much of the year as climate allows, for the maintenance of healthy soils.

Humic substances are extremely important in terms of pH buffering, inactivation of pesticides and other pollutants, improved plant nutrition and increased water-holding capacity. Humic substances can also effectively ameliorate the symptoms of dryland salinity by chelating salts and stimulating biological activity.

Bare ground, intensive tillage and the application of high rates of nitrogenous fertilisers such as urea and anhydrous ammonia, result in the loss of soil humus.

Calculating soil carbon

Soil bulk density (g/cm^3) Soil depth	1.0	1.2	1.4	1.6	1.8
0 - 10 cm	10 (37)	12 (44)	14 (51)	16 (59)	18 (66)
0 - 20 cm	20 (74)	24 (88)	28 (103)	32 (117)	36 (132)
0 - 30 cm	30 (110)	36 (132)	42 (154)	48 (176)	54 (198)

Table 1. Changes in the stock of soil carbon (tC/ha) for each 1% change in measured organic carbon status for a range of soil bulk densities and measurement depths. Numbers in brackets represent tCO2.

Soil carbon content is usually expressed as either a concentration (%) or a stock (t/ha). Unless the depth of measurement and soil bulk density parameters are known, it is not possible to accurately convert from one unit of measurement to the other.

For the sake of illustration however, some simple assumptions can be made. Changes in the stock of soil carbon (t/ha) for each 1% change in measured organic carbon status for a range of soil bulk densities and measurement depths are shown in Table 1.

Soil bulk density (g/cm^3) is the dry weight (g) of one cubic centimetre (cm^3) of soil. The higher the bulk density the more compact the soil. Generally, soils of low bulk density are well structured and have 'more space than stuff'. The lower the bulk density the more room for air and water and the better the conditions for soil life and nutrient cycling. Bulk density usually increases with soil depth. To simplify the table it was assumed that soil bulk density did not change with depth

CO_2 conversion. Every tonne of carbon lost from soil adds 3.67 tonnes of carbon dioxide (CO_2) to the atmosphere. Conversely, every 1 t/ha increase in soil organic carbon represents 3.67 tonnes of CO_2 sequestered from the atmosphere, converted to carbon compounds and stored in soil.

From the above we can see that a 1% increase in organic carbon in the top 20 cm of soil with a bulk density of 1.4 g/cm^3 represents a 28 t/ha increase in soil organic carbon, which equates to 103 t/ha of CO_2 sequestered.

These levels of increase in soil carbon are achievable, and have already been achieved, by landholders practising regenerative cropping and grazing regimes. Biological activity is concentrated in the top 10cm of most agricultural soils, but regenerative practices rapidly expand this activity to 30 cm and deeper.

The majority of the world's agricultural soils have lost enormous quantities of organic carbon, and this process needs to be reversed. What has gone up must come down. Soils, plants, animals and people will benefit when we take 're-use and recycle' to the next logical step.

Carbon and nitrogen

Nitrogen moves between the atmosphere and the topsoil in similar ways to carbon. The main difference is that the 'way in' for atmospheric carbon is via green plants whereas the 'way in' for atmospheric nitrogen is soil microbes. Soils acting as net sinks for carbon are usually also acting as net sinks for nitrogen. The flip side is that soils losing carbon are usually losing nitrogen too. In poorly aerated soils, some of this loss is in the form of nitrous oxide (N_2O), while other losses include easily leached nitrate (NO_3^-) which often takes calcium, magnesium and potassium with it, lowering the pH and creating acidic conditions.

A NEW ERA

Rewarding landholders for farming in ways that build new topsoil and raise levels of soil carbon and organic nitrogen would have a significant impact on the vitality and productivity of rural industries, while also reducing the incidence of erosion, compaction, dryland salinity and soil acidity.

As a bonus, regenerative farming practices result in the production of food much higher in vitamin and mineral content and lower in herbicide and pesticide residues than conventionally produced foods.

Any farming practice that improves soil structure is

building soil carbon. When soils become light, soft and springy, easier to dig or till and less prone to erosion, waterlogging or dryland salinity - then organic carbon levels are increasing. If soils are becoming more compact, eroded or saline - organic carbon levels are falling.

Water, energy, life, nutrients and profit will increase on-farm as soil organic carbon levels rise. The alternative is the evaporation of water, energy, life, nutrients and profit if land is mismanaged and carbon moves to the atmosphere.

It's about turning carbon loss into carbon gain.

Getting started in lifeless, compacted soils where the soil engine has shut down is the hard part. The longer we delay, the more difficult it will be to re-sequester carbon and restore vitality to the world's agricultural soils. - Dr Christine Jones

Soil Health - Historical levels of soil carbon

Polish explorer and geologist Sir Paul Edmund Strzelecki travelled widely through the colonies of south-eastern Australia during the period 1839 to 1843, visiting farms, gathering minerals, and collecting and analysing soils.

He collected forty-one soil samples from farmed paddocks of either high or low productivity. The analyses revealed the most important factor for measuring soil productivity was the level of soil carbon (measured as organic matter in the 1840s). In 1845 Strzelecki analysed forty-one samples from a wide range of soil types with the following results.

The top ten soils in the high productivity group had organic matter levels ranging from 11% to 37.75% (average 20%). The lowest ranking of ten soils in the low productivity group had organic matter levels ranging from 2.2% to 5.0% with an average of 3.72%.

Strzelecki's data indicated that soil organic matter in the early settlement period was around five to ten times higher than in most soils today, which now tests below 1% organic carbon.

Strzelecki's soil test data is consistent with reports of first settlers and early explorers who described soils in the mid-1800s as fertile and productive. The soil was also described as soft and spongy, resembling vegetable mould or what we would call compost today.

My search for more information on what was happening to Winona's soil continued. There was no interest amongst other scientists and researchers, so Dr Christine Jones and I decided to find out what changes had occurred and self-funded the collection and soil testing. We chose an area that I had changed the management to Pasture Cropping and planned grazing ten years previously, and an adjacent area that had been farmed in a conventional manner, similar to Harry's management. The samples were taken 15 meters apart and a half meter (500mm) deep on 28th September 2009

The difference in the soil tests between the two areas was astounding. Soil organic carbon had doubled. There was 90.1 tonne of carbon per hectare on Winona, and 43.41 tonnes of carbon per hectare on the adjoining paddock which is equivalent to 168.5tonnes of carbon dioxide sequestered to a depth of half a meter. The most significant increases in soil carbon occurred at depth. It doubled in the 10-20cm soil layer, tripled in the 20-30cm soil layer and quadrupled in the 30-40cm soil layer.

The relevance of this data is very important when mitigating the effects of excess CO_2 in the atmosphere and fixing the planet's changing climate.

The water-holding capacity of the soil had also increased significantly, and it now could store over 360,000 litres/ha on every rainfall event.

The soil minerals also showed remarkable increases. Calcium increased by 227%, magnesium 138%, potassium 146%, sulphur 157%, phosphorus 151%, zinc 186%, Iron 122%, copper 202%, boron 156%, molybdenum 151%, cobalt 179% and selenium 117% with the average increase in total nutrients in the Winona soil being 162 %.

This can be further explained by giving the increase in kilograms per hectare. e.g. Calcium: 12,768 kg/ha on Winona and 4,602 kg/ ha on the neighbouring paddock. Phosphorus: 837kg/ha on Winona and 554 kg/ha on the neighbouring paddock.

The results of the data collected caused very mixed reactions from people. Most farmers and graziers were very interested in the results, but a significant number of soil scientists disputed our data saying that the results were impossible and we must have 'fudged the figures'. The doubters were saying that it was not possible to increase soil carbon by as much as I had or to increase the nutrients in the soil without adding fertiliser. The data has created an academic argument around the world. Some soil scientists said it was impossible to increase soil nutrients, but others would comment and say that it was possible for two reasons. The deeper roots of the perennial grass are now sourcing nutrients from over two metres deep in the soil profile where the roots of annual pasture had not been able to reach for the last sixty years. The other source of nutrients is most likely from the parent material. The soil on Winona is of granite origin, and minerals are being released from the granite material by mycorrhizae fungi and other microbes exuding organic acids which unlock nutrients from the parent material and transport these to the plant through the fungal network.

Many scientists still doubted our results, but some people were interested in looking at the change in Winona's soil and grasslands. In 2010 Dr *Peter Ampt, Rebecca Cross, and Sarah Doornbos from the University of Sydney NSW conducted* a study on the same two paddocks where Christine, and I collected the soil samples.

The research was to evaluate the effects that different land management techniques had on the soil and farm ecosystem. The Winona paddock was Pasture Cropped with wheat in the year 2000, with oats in 2004 and with cereal rye in 2009. Since the mid-1990s the paddock and all of Winona had been grazed with a large mob of 2500 merino ewes with a grazing period of 2-3 days then allowed to recover from the graze for 90 – 120 days before re-grazing. The mob of sheep was also used to prepare the paddock for Pasture Cropping by mulching and manuring the area.

The adjacent paddock was sown to oats in the years 2000, 2004 and 2009, using traditional disc ploughing and cultivating each time the crop was sown. The sheep were grazed using traditional 'set stock' grazing (no rotation or long plant recovery time).

The only fertiliser applied to either of the paddocks during the last ten years has been with the crop when it was sown. The rates used were forty kilograms of nitrogen and phosphorus fertiliser (DAP) per hectare on Winona, and sixty kilograms of nitrogen and phosphorus fertiliser (DAP) per hectare on the adjacent paddock.

No lime had been applied to either area.

The University of Sydney recorded the results of this management.

> *Winona's paddock is now dominated by 82.9% native perennial grass species compared to 11% perennial grass and 88.1% annual species on the adjoining paddock. Winona has shown improved ecosystem, and landscape function, which is demonstrated by enhanced water infiltration improved nutrient cycling and doubling of soil nitrogen and soil carbon. The number of sheep carried on Winona is double, and crop yields are around the same. Soil microbial counts showed that the Winona soil had significantly higher counts of Fungi (46% increase) and actinomycetes bacteria (over 100% increase)*

The conclusion of the report is:

These results illustrate that the 'pasture cropping' and 'rotational grazing' practised on the site can increase perennial vegetative ground cover and litter inputs, compared to the continuous grazing system and conventional cropping practised on the comparison site. Increased perenniality and ground cover leads to improved landscape function in the pasture through increased stability, water infiltration, and nutrient cycling which in turn can result in improved soil physical and chemical properties, more growth of plants and micro-organisms and an ultimately more sustainable landscape.

It also shows that 'rotational grazing' and 'pasture cropping' can improve landscape function while sustaining similar or higher stocking rates over the year compared to the conventional system.

Even with very conclusive evidence from Sydney University research, many scientists doubted that the changes in the soil and landscape function were possible, and there must be something wrong with the data or the collection methods.

In 2009 the Soil Carbon Research Program (SCaRP) was established as part of the Climate Change Research Program within the Australian Farming Future Initiative of the Department of Agriculture, Fisheries and Forestry (DAFF).

SCaRP brought together soil carbon staff from a range of research organisations to deliver a coordinated program of research on soil carbon. The program was administered and coordinated by Australia's leading scientific organisation, the CSIRO.

The SCaRP program was invited to collect soil samples from Winona. The soil was collected to a depth of sixty centimetres in May 2011, and the results showed an increase in soil organic carbon, which was very similar to the results revealed by Sydney University and independent studies.

Scientific interest in Pasture Cropping and soil improvements did not end there.

During April to June 2013 Elizabeth Coonan from the Fenner School of Environment and Society, Australian National University, Canberra, did a study for her thesis. The study advances from previous research by comparing the interaction of Pasture Cropping to conventional cropping on soil properties using soil horizons and cover types.

Below are some extracts from Elizabeth's thesis:

Soil organic carbon (SOC), which is important for soil health, affects soil physics and nutrient cycling (Murphy, 2007). However, management practices used in conventional-cropping (CC), such as fallow periods and tillage, often reduce soil organic carbon (Luo et al., 2010). Hence, conservation management practices, such as pasture-cropping (PC), have been developed (Seis, 2009).

This study clearly demonstrates that 'pasture cropping' improves soil properties when compared to 'conventional cropping' and it should be adopted to reduce land degradation. The 'pasture cropping' site had higher total- soil organic carbon, structural stability, and nutrient concentrations in the A1–horizon and higher ground cover and landscape function over the long-term when compared to 'conventional cropping'.

Pasture cropping' maintains perennial grasses and has lower fertiliser inputs and disturbance than 'conventional cropping', leading to favourable conditions for VAM-fungi.

The soil properties under perennial grasses and litter indicate that the perennial grasses under 'pasture cropping' are affecting soil properties under both litter and grass, while the perennial grasses under 'conventional cropping' are affecting soil properties under grass only. The total- soil organic carbon strongly correlated with nutrient concentrations and weakly correlated with soil physical properties. Phosphorus concentrations are probably more limiting to carbon sequestration into stable soil organic matter pools under 'pasture cropping' than 'conventional cropping'. This may be due to the high uptake of nutrients by the continuous perennial grass sward in 'pasture cropping'.

Further, the distribution of these properties with soil horizons under 'pasture cropping' more closely resembled a natural ecosystem than 'conventional cropping'. In contrast, the 'conventional cropping' site had mixed soil horizons resulting from tillage. The potential for erosion in 'conventional cropping' may have led to nutrient loss from the A1-horizon. Additionally, the higher 'conventional cropping' fertiliser inputs may limit phosphorus mineralisation by limiting VAM-fungi numbers (Tisdall and Oades, 1982; Guppy and McLaughlin, 2009; Shen et al., 2011; Schellberg and Verbruggen, 2013). The higher aggregate stability under 'pasture cropping' than 'conventional cropping' in the A1-horizon probably results from the higher ground cover, a continuous sward of perennial grasses, and lower disturbance under 'pasture cropping' when compared to 'conventional cropping'.

The soil physical properties and nutrient cycling results indicate that perennial grasses in 'pasture cropping' extend beyond the plant basal area, increasing structural stability and lowering bulk density under both perennial grasses and litter.

In contrast, the perennial grasses under 'conventional cropping', which are removed prior to cropping, did not appear to be affecting soil physical properties under litter. Further, the litter under 'conventional cropping' appeared to be adding organic nutrients to the soil, while in 'pasture cropping' perennial grass maintenance promoted uptake of phosphorus and nitrogen from under both perennial grasses and litter through VAM-fungi, rhizobia, and root exudates. This resulted in similar nutrient concentrations under grass and litter in 'pasture cropping.' - Elizabeth Coonan

Data collected from the many research projects on Winona has produced almost the same results. As well as growing excellent crops for grain and animal forage, Pasture Cropping will increase perennial pasture species and species diversity, soil organic carbon, soil structure, soil microbial numbers and diversity, nutrient availability and nutrient cycling.

These results are remarkable but have been achieved using simple methods that almost anyone can do. It is the diverse grassland that is driving most of the positive results. Managed well, the grasslands supply complete groundcover of litter, which conserve moisture, control weeds, feed decomposer soil microbes and maintain relatively constant ground temperature for optimal soil microbe health and plant health. The grassland vegetation also supplies root exudates which provide food to soil microbes. The pasture crop of oats or wheat, which is sown into the grassland, when it is at its dormant stage in winter continues the supply of root exudates and fuels the soil ecosystem with more energy, feeding mycorrhizal fungi and other soil microbes during a period of reduced, grassland plant growth.

Sheep grazing in large mobs through the paddocks every three to four months add a pulse of nutrients with dung and urine, trample and mulch the grassland and prune the roots of the grass.

This regenerative system creates a positive feedback loop, which stimulates the recruitment of more perennial plants, further restoring the grassland, improving nutrient cycling, and increasing soil nutrients, which in turn increases soil microbe diversity and enhances the soil and farm ecosystem.

✇ 8 ✇

INDUSTRIALISED AGRICULTURE

L ike the industrial revolution that occurred in
England and Europe in the mid-1700s, the so-called
'green agricultural revolution' which started in the
late 1940s had good and bad consequences.

Harry adopted parts of the green revolution, like many
farmers of that era. The use of new varieties of wheat and oats
increased grain yields from the 1950s, and some of the shorter
stemmed wheat varieties were a significant advantage
because there were fewer problems with crops lodging, or
falling onto the ground toward the end of the season. Lodging
and tangled crops are challenging to harvest, and often
severely lodged crops cannot be harvested at all. The
improvement in new higher yielding pasture species like
many of the sub clover and ryegrass varieties improved
production while ever fertiliser was added to them. Harry,
fortunately, did not adopt any of the herbicides that were
being promoted during that era, preferring to plough soil to
grow crops and cultivate weeds before sowing the crop. He
did, however, find it necessary to use insecticides like DDT to
control insects that invaded the crops and pasture.

Before the end of the 1970s, the wheels were starting to fall off Winona. The increasing price of fertiliser was starting to make its use unaffordable, but it was essential to continue to apply nutrients to the phosphorus and nitrogen dependent wheat, oats and pasture plants that were grown during this era. We were locked into a method of farming that required an annual fix of fertiliser, and the unhealthy crops and pastures became an attractant to insects that required increasing doses of insecticide to control. We were on a downward financial and ecological spiral that was almost impossible to get out of. Production from crops and sheep were dependent on increasing inputs of chemicals and veterinary products that were necessary because of the way agriculture had evolved. It had come to a point where the manufacturers of the products were becoming wealthy, and farmers were going broke.

The Green Revolution can no longer be afforded. Modern industrialised, chemical agriculture relies on vast amounts of oil and gas that are used as raw materials and energy to produce fertilisers and pesticides, and as cheap and readily available energy for all stages of food production. The modern, agriculture method that feeds much of the world is entirely dependent on the processing and distribution of cheap crude oil, which is destined to be in short supply sometime in the future.

Even though crop yields in the Western world have increased threefold since the start of the green revolution, the energy input to agriculture has increased fourfold and energy by way of fossil fuels must continue to grow to maintain current crop yields. Modern industrialised agriculture is using more energy with the use of oil and gas than the energy from food that it is producing. It is also very concerning when we look at how the quantity of oil extracted since 1981 has exceeded discoveries by an ever-widening margin. In 2008, the world produced 31 billion barrels of oil but discovered fewer than 9 billion barrels of new oil.

Nature will always win, and it was less than twenty years since the start of the Green Revolution when she began to fight back. Insects were developing resistance to many of the insecticides, and weeds were becoming resistant to herbicides.

The first case of herbicide resistance in the United States was reported in the 1950s. In Kansas during 1964 bindweed had become resistant to the highly effective broad-leaf herbicide 2, 4-D, and resistance to triazine herbicides was discovered in Washington in 1970.

In Australia, herbicide-resistant populations of annual ryegrass and wild oats were first identified in the early 1980s, and within ten years, the problem had become widespread.

Modern chemical-based agriculture retaliated by declaring war on weeds and insects with companies developing even more potent herbicides and applying insecticides at higher and higher rates was costing the farmer more and more money.

The amount of pesticide now being used worldwide is alarming, with over half a million tonnes of active ingredient applied annually to crops and pasture, but despite the enormous amount of pesticide used, the yearly loss of crops due to pests still exceeds thirty percent.

The failure of pesticides is clarified in an international survey of herbicide-resistant weeds done in 2013. It showed there are currently over four hundred cases of herbicide resistant weeds globally, which have developed resistance to one hundred and forty-eight different herbicides, in sixty-one countries.

The increase in pesticides started to ring alarm bells with ecologists and a small band of scientists who began to criticise the intensity of chemical inputs, saying that it reduced soil fertility, genetic diversity, and created long-term vulnerability to pests. Of course, the comments were dismissed as alarmist, and life went on as before, with companies producing more pesticides and farmers applying them.

. . .

HUMAN HEALTH

The Green Revolution was not only involved in the production and use of pesticides and producing high yielding crops to produce more food, but it was also engaged in creating a global food system dedicated to expanding the industrialisation of agriculture.

Within 20 years from the start of the Green Revolution, human health problems were starting to arise. Extended exposure to pesticides such as organochlorines, sulphate, and creosote were linked to increased cancer rates, and DDT, chlordane, and lindane connected with tumours. Just as significant as the rise in cancer and tumours since the start of the Green Revolution is the change of nutrients in food during the same period. A paper titled 'A Study of the Mineral Depletion of Foods' published in *Nutrition and Health* in 2003 and written by McCance & Widdowson, provides the most detailed and sophisticated historical records for Britain of the nutrient values of foods available to any nation worldwide.

The conclusions in this paper are frightening and are associated with the way food is grown. A summary of the results shows the percentage decrease in minerals that is essential for human health, during the time of the Green Revolution from 1940 to 2003. These results showed the average changes in seventy-two food products, which included vegetables, fruit, meat, and dairy. Sodium was reduced by 34%, Potassium reduced by 15%, Magnesium reduced by 19%, Calcium reduced by 29%, Iron reduced by 37%, and Copper reduced by a massive 62%.

Another study was done on mineral depletion done by Donald Davis and his team of researchers from the University of Texas. They studied the U.S. Department of Agriculture's nutritional data from both 1950 and 1999 for forty-three different vegetables and fruits. The results, published in December 2004 in the Journal of the American College of Nutrition, showed a severe decline of protein, calcium, phosphorus, iron, riboflavin (vitamin B2) and vitamin C, over the previous half-century.

In Australia during 2008, the leading scientific research organisation, the CSIRO, found that adding phosphate fertiliser to a wheat crop reduced zinc levels in wheat grains by thirty-three to thirty-nine percent. This has the potential to cause zinc deficiency in people who get most of their zinc from wheat in their diet. The research suggested phosphate destroyed the main soil microbe, arbuscular mycorrhizal fungi, which sourced zinc and many other nutrients for the wheat plant. Long fallows and canola crops, which can also reduce mycorrhizal fungi, produced a similar depletion of zinc in wheat grains.

In healthy ecosystems plants work in symbiosis with soil microbes and that relationship increases the transfer of essential nutrients from the soil to plant. The nutrients in the plant then become available to us either directly through grain like wheat, or via animals that eat the nutrient-rich plants.

The impact of poor nutrition on health has long been common knowledge. Herbal treatment for scurvy has been used in many cultures since prehistory. Scurvy was documented as a disease by the ancient Greek physician Hippocrates, and the Ancient Egyptians recorded its symptoms as early as 1550 BC. As long ago as the mid-1700s it was known that a lack of fruit and vegetables caused scurvy, but it was not until 1905 that Englishman William Fletcher discovered that if specific factors (vitamins) were removed from food, the disease occurred.

When my ancestor William Moor and 299 of his fellow convicts were cast aboard the transport ship for their journey to Australia in 1799, the Government of the day were aware that a lack of fruit and vegetables caused scurvy and the convicts and crew were to be fed vegetables to prevent the disease. Even though they were only given cabbage, the cabbage was enough to prevent scurvy and keep 257 of them alive during their 181-day journey.

For more than a hundred years, we have known about vitamin deficiency diseases. Only recently the importance of the health of the soil in which our food is growing has been realised.

There can be many reasons why food today has substantially fewer vitamins and minerals. Breeding varieties of crops for their presentation rather than nutritional quality and increased transport distances, storage times, and storage methods for 'fresh' produce can all affect food quality.

The most compelling reason for vitamin and mineral decline in food is soil depletion: Modern agricultural methods have stripped increasing amounts of nutrients from the soil, in which our food grows. Monoculture crops and the overuse of chemical fertiliser and pesticides contribute to nutrient-depleted soil and their resulting damage to soil microbes that help release and cycle essential minerals from the soil and make them available to plants.

Research from many parts of the world has confirmed the loss of micronutrients from our food and showed evidence that vitamin and mineral deficiencies significantly affect our health. Even with this knowledge, the farming methods known to contribute to a decline in mineral depletion of our soils continue with the unrelenting pursuit of agriculture and marketing practices that emphasise cheapness over quality.

We must do better and start to use agricultural methods that create healthy microbial rich soil instead of practices that continue to apply excessive levels of pesticides and chemical fertiliser that do considerable damage to the soil structure, soil health and ultimately human health.

But how do we change and what can we change to?

It is very easy to blame the growers of the food, the world's farmers, but farmers are only trying to make a living like everyone else and are often innocent bystanders in the Green Revolution. In many instances, farmers have been manipulated by companies with financial interests in selling the new products of seed, fertiliser and pesticides they have developed.

Yes, the Green Revolution has produced more food. Yes, the green revolution has made farming easier. But what has this cost us? We now have soils all over the world that have lost soil structure, lost in some cases 80% of their carbon, lost water holding capacity, and lost most of their nutrients. In other words, much of the planet has become dysfunctional and incapable of supplying food of sufficient nutrient density for human consumption. It should be no surprise why it has now become necessary for people to take vitamin and mineral supplements.

Monoculture Cropping

For almost one hundred years it has been known that fertiliser requirement for crops, weed management, grain quality, and harvesting could be better managed if cereal crops are grown as a single species. This became more apparent with the development of herbicides for weed control that could be used before sowing the crop and selective herbicides that would kill weeds amongst the crop.

Monoculture cropping had never been practised on such a large scale until the latter part of the Green Revolution. By the end of the 20th century, many millions of acres were being planted over vast areas to one species, and now over ninety percent of the world's 1.5 billion hectares of crops such as wheat, corn, and soybean are planted in monocultures. This method of growing crops relies on extensive use of large amounts of fertiliser to replace lost nutrients and the application of pesticides, which are necessary to limit the high levels of crop damage that inevitably occur.

There are however some advantages of crop monocultures, and the greatest is the capacity to produce massive amounts of grain very efficiently. This is achieved with specialised machinery for pesticide application and large, efficient seeding and harvesting equipment.

Is it possible to continue with this method of growing crops? Their very design requires ever increasing fertiliser, insecticide, fungicide and herbicide, of which their source is a finite resource. Couple this with the environmental and ecological damage that is being done to the planet's terrestrial and soil ecosystems and human health, we should be asking how long these techniques can continue.

Nature does not function as a monoculture. In natural systems like grasslands, there are hundreds of plant species which are complemented by vast numbers and a huge diversity of insects, birds and animals. The soil beneath grassland is also very diverse in life with bacteria, fungi, protozoa, nematodes and earthworms that are so abundant that a spoonful of healthy grassland soil contains almost as many organisms as there are humans on the planet. Natural systems rarely suffer from disease or out of control insect attack. The vast range of species keeps pests under control. For example, spiders in grassland control insects that damage plants and the diverse soil life control plant root disease by preventing any one microbe species from increasing in numbers to such an extent that they harm plants. These examples reflect aspects of natural controls that maintain most native ecosystems in a state of sound stability.

It should not come as a surprise that modern monoculture cropping systems are failing because of crop disease, insect attack and declining soil nutrients. Industrialised cropping methods have destroyed the ecosystem that is essential for plants to grow, and while ever there are cropping systems that are propped up with excessive pesticides and chemical fertiliser, it will continue to fail.

Around the world, much of the soil in which crops are grown was originally formed by the planet's vast grasslands over tens of thousands of years. These soils have lost one-half of their topsoil after farming for less than 100 years and are eroding 30 times faster than the natural formation rate. These once exceptionally fertile soils are now little more than a medium to hold a plant upright and a sponge into which we must pour very high levels of chemical fertilisers to produce crops.

The Green Revolution that started in the late 1940s and showed such great promise for feeding the world, and being free of insect attack and weeds, has been a failure because it never accounted for the natural function of ecosystems. If it continues in the same manner without incorporating natural systems, it will always be plagued with ecological problems.

THE NEXT GREEN REVOLUTION

By the end of the 20th century, many people were becoming more aware of the looming difficulty in feeding the planet's predicted nine billion people by the middle of the twenty-first century. As more problems with crop disease, insects and declining soil emerged, the Green Revolution that was developed to feed the world's growing population was failing, and other ways of growing more food were required. Instead of looking at different approaches, like improving food distribution, slowing world population growth, or more importantly developing a regenerative form of agriculture, improving the existing failed model with genetically modified crops and better pesticides is seen as the way to solve our problems.

During the 1980s there was growing awareness of the environmental and human health concerns associated with foliar-applied organophosphate insecticides, and a search began to find a safer insecticide. Nicotine has been used as an insecticide for over 200 years, but it degraded too rapidly in the environment and was not suitable in large-scale agricultural situations. In an effort to solve this problem, neonicotinoids were developed as a substitute of nicotine and in 1991 the first neonicotinoid compound, imidacloprid, was launched by Bayer CropScience.

Neonicotinoids are systemic insecticides that are the synthetic versions of nicotine. Unlike contact insecticides, which remain on the surface of the plant foliage, systemic insecticides are taken up by the plant and transported into the leaves, flowers, roots stems, pollen and nectar of the plant. The product can be applied by spraying onto the crop foliage or as seed coating that spreads from the seed throughout the plant, which protects the crop by disrupting the nervous system of any insect which eats the plant.

Neonicotinoids have become widely adopted around the world because of their effectiveness in controlling pests and their ease of application. Treating seed with insecticide is seen as a more efficient method of targeting pests than spraying crop foliage and more environmentally friendly because it can reduce the number of spray applications needed in the field. This made the product safer to use, and the systemic action made it persistent in crops and soil which extended the time it would control insects. Because of these benefits, neonicotinoids are now one of the most widely used insecticides in the world.

The new systemic insecticide was seen as a major scientific breakthrough, and it looked as though scientists had created a perfect pesticide that would control insects and was safer for humans, livestock and birds than any previous insecticide. However, over time, some insidious problems started to arise with this apparently safe insecticide as it has become apparent that it posed different and poorly understood risks to non-target beneficial insects such as bees.

Insects are often regarded as being of no benefit and seen as an annoying nuisance or a serious problem because they destroy crops, but a reduction in insect diversity could have serious ecological consequences. Without insects, many of the world's plants could not exist, and our food supply would be decimated because insects pollinate seventy percent of the world's food crops. Without insects, much of the world's bird population would be severely reduced because insects are a main source of food for many of them. Killing insects without taking into account the ecology could have unforeseen and potentially catastrophic consequences. Influencing natural insect control may make insect attack on crops worse, which would necessitate the use of more insecticides.

When first introduced, neonicotinoids were believed to have a low level of toxicity to many insects, but current research has shown they are one of the most toxic groups of chemicals and will kill bees and other beneficial insects even at extremely low levels. The extensive use of neonicotinoids in many cropping systems and its unexpected occurrence in pollen and nectar has also created a significant problem for pollinators. Neonicotinoids are creating a severe decline in ecosystems with the loss of insects and birds, but perhaps the more urgent issue is that the insecticide is being implicated in the death of bees. Neonicotinoids are considered a significant factor in 'colony collapse disorder' and has been shown to induce acute and chronic effects with up to 90% of bees dying in some areas.

In April 2015 The European Academies Science Advisory Council (EASAC) did a study on the potential effects organisms have by providing a range of ecosystem services like pollination and natural pest control which are critical to sustainable agriculture The concluding report stated "there is an increasing body of evidence that the widespread use of

neonicotinoids has severe adverse effects on non-target
organisms that provide ecosystem services including
pollination and natural pest control

In the July 2014 issue of the journal *Nature*, a study based
on an observed correlation between declines in some bird
populations and the use of neonicotinoid pesticides in the
Netherlands demonstrated that the level of neonicotinoids
detected in environmental samples correlated strongly with
the decline in populations of insect-eating birds. An editorial
published in the same edition found the possible link between
neonicotinoid pesticide use and a decline in bird numbers
"worrying", pointing out that the persistence of the
compounds and the low direct toxicity to birds themselves
implies that the depletion of the birds' food source (insects) is
likely responsible for the decline and that the compounds are
distributed widely in the environment.

It has been suggested that the world needs a better and
safer insecticide to protect crops from insect attack. But this
approach is a serious part of the problem. More insecticides
are not going to solve the problem of insects. Insects are not
the problem; insect attack of crops is a symptom of the
agricultural methods we are using. The only long-term
answer to this problem is to have and a balanced, diverse
ecosystem with more insects, birds, wildlife, and plant
diversity. We already have the best possible method of insect
control. Mother Nature controls insects with ecosystems with
a diverse range of plants that attract a diverse variety of
insects. The wide variety of insects includes a balance of
beneficial insects like predatory wasps and spiders that
control crop and pasture damaging insects.

GENETICALLY MODIFIED ORGANISMS

The World Health Organisation defines genetically
modified organisms (GMOs) as "organisms in which the

genetic material (DNA) has been altered in a way that does not occur naturally", but the term is commonly used for crops that have been genetically modified to produce a desired trait. When incorporated into the DNA of an organism, genetically engineered genes alter the characteristics of an organism.

Genetically modified crops have been promoted to have the potential to reduce insecticide and herbicide use, increase water efficiency, tolerate adverse growing conditions and improve yields. The most common traits in genetically modified crops currently on the market are designed to kill insects that try to eat a plant or to make the crop tolerant to the herbicide.

A bacteria called Bacillus thuringiensis **(Bt)** is a naturally occurring, soil-borne bacteria that produces a protein called Bt toxin. The toxin is used by bacteria as a natural defence and uses it to fend off insect larvae, predators, and other pathogens. When specific insects consume the bacterium, the toxin is released in the insect's gut, and the insect dies.

Bacillus thuringiensis (Bt) was first discovered in 1901 by Japanese biologist Ishiwata Shigetane. It was rediscovered in Germany by Ernst Berliner, who found it was the cause of a disease that killed flour moth caterpillars and in 1961 developed and registered as a biological pesticide in the U.S.A. after it was found to be an excellent and safe method of insect control. The insecticides produced by Bt bacteria are non contact poisons and must be eaten by the insect lava to be effective. There seem to be no adverse effects on non-target organisms when exposed to Bt, and the consequences on the environment are considered mild because when exposed to higher temperatures and sunlight, Bt spores start deteriorating soon after it is sprayed.

Bt is the most common environmentally-friendly insecticide used and is the basis of almost 200 registered products on the market today. It has been used for decades as a safe insecticidal spray in chemically-based, and organic farming. This success encouraged genetic engineers to genetically modify plants to be resistant to insect attack by inserting the DNA from *Bacillus thuringiensis into them.*

Corn was first genetically engineered in 1996 to kill the European corn borer and related species by using sections of the DNA from *Bacillus thuringiensis. The DNA* is isolated and inserted into the plant cells by a process known as genetic transformation. The plant is then regenerated from transgenic plant cells, and the entire plant becomes an insecticide. When an insect eats the plant, the insect's gut wall breaks down, allowing toxin and gut bacteria to enter the insect's body and the insect dies.

Using naturally occurring insecticide and inserting it into a plant was seen as an important breakthrough in pest control, reducing the need to spray insecticides. Genetically modified crops are engineered to produce the insecticide Bt toxin, which was assumed to contain the same safe insecticidal toxin as the natural form. The natural toxin has been shown to be safe over decades of use; it only affects certain types of insects, and thought to be harmless to humans and other mammals. Because of this, it was assumed that genetically modified crops, engineered to contain Bt insecticidal toxin, must also be safe, but over time, its human and ecological safety is coming into question.

Natural Bt toxin has been found to be different from the Bt toxins produced in genetically modified crops and behaves differently in the environment because natural Bt toxin has a different mode of action from the Bt toxin produced in genetically engineered plants. Natural Bt is not a toxin but a protoxin, which means it only becomes toxic under certain conditions. The protoxin is contained within the bacterium and is not toxic until an insect eats it. The Bt gene inserted into genetically-modified corn only contains the toxin without its bacterial containment.

With genetically modified Bt crops, the plant itself

becomes a pesticide. Every cell of the plant contains the toxin in pre-activated form, and people and animals that eat the plant are also eating a pesticide.

Animal feeding experiments with genetically modified Bt crops have revealed toxic effects, and a laboratory study showed toxic effects on human cells. Bt toxin has been shown to not reliably break down in the digestive tract of humans, and toxin proteins have been found circulating in the blood of pregnant women and the blood supply of their unborn children.

The use of genetically modified Bt crops appear to reduce pesticide use because crops are not sprayed as often with chemical insecticides, but genetically modified Bt crops do not reduce insecticides. They merely change the type of insecticide and the way in which it is used, from sprayed on to built in. Claims that genetically modified Bt crops reduce insecticide use fail to take into account the fact that the genetically engineered Bt crop is itself an insecticide. The amount of modified Bt toxin expressed in the plant is far greater than the amount of chemical pesticide displaced, and pollen from Bt crop has been shown to have toxic effects on non-target insects and beneficial organisms.

Plants are also genetically modified to be tolerant to herbicide by identifying micro-organisms that are tolerant of the active chemical in the herbicide. These are inserted into the plant's genes by a process that results in a plant that can resist the direct application of the herbicide.

Glyphosate is the most widely used herbicide in the world and has been used extensively in over one hundred and sixty countries for many years. Marketed as Roundup and other trade names, glyphosate is a broad-spectrum systemic herbicide which is regarded as an excellent weed killer that will kill almost any plant.

The herbicide has been used for decades to control weeds before a crop is sown. It could not be applied to a crop that had weeds amongst it because the herbicide would also kill the crop.

To solve this problem, soybeans and corn were genetically modified to be tolerant to glyphosate, and commercialised in the U.S.A. in 1996. Now soybeans and corn crops could be sprayed with glyphosate, enabling weeds to be controlled without killing the crop. The adoption of herbicide-tolerant soybeans was dramatic, with a million acres of the soybeans sown in the first year. Now approximately 95 percent of soybean and more than 85 percent of corn in the USA are planted to varieties genetically modified to be herbicide resistant.

GM technology has been widely adopted around the world. The area sown to genetically modified crops now includes 12% of global cropland, increasing from 1.7 million hectares the late 1990s to 185.1 million hectares in 2016.

When plants were first genetically engineered, glyphosate-resistant enzymes were isolated from a strain of Agrobacterium. Agrobacterium has been known as a plant pathogen since the beginning of the 20th century, being discovered to cause a tumour in plants called 'crown gall' disease. In recent years comprehensive research has been done on this bacterium's method of tumour induction, which was found to be made by transferring a small segment of DNA into the host plant cell. However during the last few decades, the capacity of Agrobacterium to transfer DNA to plant cells been exploited for genetic engineering.

Crops that have been genetically modified for tolerance to glyphosate have made it possible to spray herbicide on a growing crop. This development has made it easier and more efficient to control weeds, but not without cost.

Herbicide-tolerant crops performed extremely well in the first few years of use, but over-reliance and overuse of glyphosate have led to weeds that are resistant to glyphosate, which cannot be killed with the herbicide. The industry solution to the herbicide-resistant weeds has been to use more herbicides. In the USA this has led to an increase of 25% of herbicide used each year, which has grown from 680 thousand kilograms in 1999 to over 40 million kilograms in 2011. The widespread use of GM crops and overuse of herbicide has seen glyphosate-resistant weeds expand to 61.2 million acres in recent years

The potential of biotechnology to create human health and environment problems is hotly debated, but it does not change the fact that crops which are genetically modified for herbicide resistance, are sprayed with herbicides which eventually get into the human food chain. The herbicide ends up in food because crops are sprayed directly with herbicides. The herbicide-resistant plants absorb the herbicide and the plant or seed that contains the herbicide is eaten.

Since the development of herbicides, many have been promoted as safe for humans, animals and the environment. Most, if not all, herbicides are toxic. When glyphosate was first developed it was believed to be safe and promoted as safe to use, but glyphosate's toxicity has been underestimated.

Commercial glyphosate herbicide formulations contain added ingredients which are more toxic than glyphosate alone, and independent studies have shown toxic effects of glyphosate include disruption of human hormonal systems, damage to DNA, developmental toxicity, birth defects, cancer, neurotoxicity and changes to beneficial gut bacteria.

In March 2015, the World Health Organisation's research division, the 'International Agency for Cancer Research' (IARC), reviewed its cancer evaluation on a list of herbicides and insecticides and the herbicide glyphosate and the insecticides malathion and diazinon were classified as probably carcinogenic to humans.

The developers of genetically modified plants claim that food from these plants is "identical to non-genetically modified plants." They argue that genetic engineering is no different to plant hybridisation and plant breeding, which has been practised for centuries, but genetic engineering is very different from traditional plant breeding.

With the use of genetic engineering, organisms can be given combinations of new traits that do not occur in nature and cannot be created by natural means. This attitude to breeding is nothing like traditional plant breeding, which is done by selecting for traits over many generations of the plant. Traditional breeding does not select for genes whereas biotechnology targets the genes, which influence traits of the plant.

The problem with this is that genes that are being inserted into plants could never have occurred there naturally, and the long-term consequences of this are unknown. Many of these new plants and food produced from them are being put into the world without the necessary safeguards, and no scientist can be certain that food produced from genetically modified crops are without risk. Until the risks are known, a vast majority of the world's human and animal population is being subjected to an enormous feeding experiment.

Genetically modified crops have been promoted as a solution to the world's food shortage problems, and much of the despair afflicting agriculture, but it does not treat the cause of agriculture's predicament. Genetically modified crops are promoted to improve yield, drought tolerance, food quality and fertiliser efficiency, but the only traits yet produced are herbicide tolerance and insect resistance. Genetically modified crop yields have not increased because they were not developed to give higher yields and usually produce no more than the traditionally bred parent crop. Genetically modified crop technology is also breaking down under the pressure of herbicide-resistant weeds and pests resistant to the Bt toxin engineered into crops.

In an attempt to revolutionise agriculture, the same economic interests that developed the first chemical-based

Green Revolution are now endorsing biotechnology and genetic engineering. Promoted as the 'Next Green Revolution', in reality they are promoting genetic engineering to fix the problems created by the original Green Revolution and are using a technological solution to repair agricultural disasters that are environmental and ecological problems.

The agrochemical corporations who are developing genetically engineered crops claim that their technology will enhance agriculture's sustainability by solving problems created by modern agriculture and the Green Revolution. It is often publicised that the adoption of their advanced technology will, increase yields, reduce insect attack, decrease pesticide use and increase profit. These are the same claims that were being made during the original Green Revolution in the 1950s and 1960s. The genetic engineering industry's real motivation is not to make agriculture more productive and create more profit for farmers, but to generate profits for the company that developed the technology.

Genetically engineering plants and animals is not solving the problems of agriculture and can make our problems worse. There are other ways of producing large amounts of food while restoring farms, ecosystems and the planet. There is clearly a long way to go, but growing numbers of farmers in all countries of the world are changing agriculture. They use regenerative farming methods that are restoring soil, increasing soil organic carbon, water holding capacity, increasing soil nutrients, and producing large quantities of nutrient-rich food.

Is Science Being Censored?

For many years, the general public has thought that the complete truth about agricultural science and scientific developments may not be fully told. It has also been suggested that companies that have developed a technology or chemical could be influencing science and scientific research. There are many instances where scientists have been told to keep quiet about their research data and been instructed not to speak publicly about their findings.

Dr Maarten Stapper is an Australian agricultural scientist with more than thirty years of international experience. He worked for twenty-three years for the Commonwealth Scientific and Industrial Research Organisation (CSIRO) which is the federal government agency for scientific research in Australia. Dr Stapper worked in southeastern Australia as a farming systems research agronomist and received The Fellowship of the Australian Institute of Agricultural Science and Technology (FAIAST) award for his dedicated service.

Since the early development of genetic engineering, Dr Stapper was sceptical about claims that genetically modified plants improved crop yields, and he called for more studies on the safety of genetically modified crops. Those comments attracted the attention of CSIRO executives, and Dr Stapper claimed that senior CSIRO management tried to stop his criticisms of genetically modified crops through harassment and bullying.

The CSIRO stopped him from continuing with biologic-organic farming research, and Dr Stapper was forced to leave in March 2007, when his position with CSIRO's plant industry division was made redundant.

In the USA Dr Jonathan Lundgren worked for the United States Department of Agriculture (USDA) Agricultural Research (ARS) for more than a decade as Senior Research Entomologist. He is a respected expert on the risk assessment of pesticides and genetically modified crops.

Dr Lundgren researched neonicotinoid insecticides and their effect on beneficial insects. His study showed that the insecticide application killed non-target insects and that the pesticide was found in milkweed plants, which are the only food source for the developing larvae of monarch butterflies.

Dr Lundgren has also published papers suggesting that soybean seeds pre-treated with neonicotinoid pesticide produce no yield benefit to farmers. He also presented a paper on potential hazards with the latest development in genetic engineering, "gene silencing" pesticides (RNAi), which he said required further study to determine whether they could harm other organisms.

His progressive research has drawn worldwide attention, but when his research on the consequences of systemic pesticides and RNAi on pollinators began to gain momentum, the USDA suspended Dr Lundgren and tried to prevent him from speaking about his conclusions. The suspension affected his personnel file, harmed his reputation, and cost him over $9,000 in lost pay and expenses. Dr Lundgren is not alone; other scientists have been ordered to retract studies, water-down findings, and otherwise hushed and harassed. They just haven't come forward.

Both Dr Maarten Stapper and Dr Jonathon Lundgren have been victims of science that is not independent. Science should be about finding the truth, not hiding the truth.

Science is often not impartial. Many organisations and universities who conduct research are indirectly funded by powerful corporate donors. As a result, many studies are controlled by the companies that develop and manufacture the products under study, but having these companies in charge of the research is like putting the fox in charge of the hen house.

Dr Jonathan Lundgren has now left the United States Department of Agriculture and has set up his own research farm in South Dakota called Blue Dasher Farms. The research farm is designed to supply independent and honest research that will connect science with innovative farmers in what will hopefully become a United States national centre of excellence in regenerative agriculture.

Dr Maarten Stapper now spends his time speaking about soil health and biological farming practices, educating, and consulting with farmers on how to transition from conventional to biological and organic farming systems.

❧ 9 ❧

WORLD AGRICULTURE

*O*ur current world industrialised agriculture and
economic system has lifted billions of people worldwide
out of hunger and poverty and created a standard of
living that people could have only dreamt about. Regrettably, most
people and politicians cannot see the problems and are very happy to
proceed with, what they believe to be an excellent and successful
worldwide system. Its success is also a significant part of the
problem. The manner in which it has been successful, with the
exploitation of nature and the need for continual growth is what is
driving us past the point of no return. Human greed and the urge to
produce more farming land has created worldwide deforestation and
expanding agriculture into low rainfall, marginal areas, are causing
desertification. This relentless materialistic approach is creating the
inevitable destruction of the world ecosystems, which, if continued
impossible to recover.

Alan Savory has been instrumental in developing grazing
management strategies that mimic natural grazing behaviour
of wild animals, but crops have been grown by creating
conditions that would never happen in nature. Mother Nature
very rarely allows large areas of soil to be bare and

212

uncovered. She heals the area by quickly colonising it with fast-growing annual plants that we call weeds.

Most of the problems associated with growing crops are caused by crop growing methods, which are far removed from natural systems. The ground preparation method to plant crops is done either by ploughing the soil or killing all living plants with herbicide. The monoculture crop planted into the bare soil is the opposite of what happens with native grasslands where a diverse range of colonising plants is set to work to cover and heal the soil. On cropping farms, large areas are grown as single species monoculture crops, and between crop seasons the soil is kept bare. It then becomes necessary for the soil ecosystem to be propped up with increasing amounts of chemical fertiliser and pesticides. As the soil ecosystems collapse more and more colonising plants invade the area, putting increasing pressure on the herbicides that are used to control them. This problem has been attempted to be solved by developing genetically modified plants to be tolerant to the herbicide, which makes it more efficient to kill the weeds. As soil becomes even more dysfunctional, it loses carbon and its associated ability to hold water, then plants struggle to grow because of insufficient soil water. To address this potential crisis, plants are being genetically modified to be resistant to drought. As the farm ecosystem collapses and crop-damaging insects increase, the problem is then solved by genetically changing plants to be tolerant to insect attack.

Rural Decline

The problems with Industrial agriculture never seem to end. One of the more insidious industrial agriculture outcomes is the decline of rural towns and the loss of communities worldwide. One has only to drive through many rural areas to see the sad reality of what industrial agriculture has created.

Fifty to sixty years ago, when driving through a rural landscape in Australia's mixed farming areas, you would observe a different scene.

The farms would consist of a diversity of enterprises, comprised of sheep, cattle and crops of wheat and oats. The houses and buildings were well kept, having an air of pride and success. People were employed on the farms to tend the animals, grow crops and maintain the property.

Today, I often have the opportunity, or I should say, reluctance to drive through many hundreds of kilometres of rural areas to see and feel the destruction this form of industrial agriculture enforces upon the land. There are dead and dying trees, windswept dry, dusty paddocks, no sheep or cattle, no birds, no wildlife, and depressing, fallen down, unlived houses. Not even the houses and trees have survived in some areas, having been bulldozed, burned and buried to make way for more land to grow crops.

Not only are the farms destroyed, but the guts have been sucked out of the rural towns.

Gone are the sporting teams, gone are the schools, gone are the people, banks and the local doctor. The town is now a derelict ruin, with many of the houses unoccupied and falling into disrepair.

How can an agricultural practice cause such devastation?

This form of agriculture attracts large companies who are only interested in making money. They do this by first buying the small farms then, over time, larger farms until they own vast areas of land. To make the crop growing enterprise as cost-efficient as possible huge machinery is used, and very little labour employed, compared to what the small farms used to hire. Almost nothing is purchased in the local town. Even the districts produce supplier is no longer needed as vast quantities of fertiliser, herbicides and pesticides are trucked in to make their operation as efficient as possible.

In a faraway city, the money-hungry board of directors, who have no connection to the land, and do not care about the farm or the rural community's loss, drive the final nail in the coffin.

As their industrial farming methods destroy the soil and the extensive farm's ecosystem, the crop yields decline, and their vast operation becomes unprofitable. The company sells the now useless land and moves on to destroy another rural community.

Food

Directly associated with a decline in the soil ecosystem is the quality of food that is produced from the nutrient-depleted soil. Food grown in this soil is also low in nutrients, which is a primary reason for the increasing human health crisis occurring around the world. Biotechnology is solving the predicament of food depleted in nutrients in its usual way. Modify the plant, and not change the manner in which food is grown.

A crisis has emerged in Asia where children are suffering from a diet-related vitamin A deficiency, which can lead to blindness. This problem has attempted to be solved by genetically modifying rice to be rich in beta-carotene, or vitamin A. The dilemma is not rice but the manner in which rice is now grown. In more recent years agricultural practices in much of Asia have changed from diverse agriculture to rice monoculture promoted by the green revolution and industrial agriculture. Biotechnology is attempting to fix a problem that that is related to declining diversity in the food, which is caused by industrial agriculture.

The troubles do not end with growing crops; a similar predicament occurs when Pasture is re-sown. Most re-sown

Pasture is selected with little regard for species diversity, and production being the primary consideration. This type of Pasture does not even vaguely resemble the original grassland ecosystem, and because of this, requires ever-increasing amounts of fertiliser to maintain its production, and pesticide is necessary to manage pest and disease that continue to attack it.

When are we going to understand that the problem lies in how crops and Pasture are grown? An increasing amount of chemical fertiliser, pesticides and genetic engineering are being used to fix the disasters of the original 'green revolution'.

MOUSE AND LOCUST PLAGUES

As Eastern Australia and Winona emerge out of one of the most severe droughts ever recorded within a year, it was followed by one of the worst mouse plagues in living memory in 2021. There are reports and film of mice invading towns by the millions, devastating sorghum crops and destroying hundreds of thousands of dollars worth of stored grain and hay. This has been devastating for many people, especially after years of severe drought.

Interestingly, the mouse numbers have not been the same everywhere. Some farms, including Winona, have not had the mouse numbers or the impact on farm livelihood. Why?

Over many years locust plagues have caused similar destruction of crops, pasture and livelihood. Both mice and locust plagues often occur after droughts when they are followed by years of good rainfall. Locusts require bare soil to lay their eggs, which is plentiful during drought years. The eggs lay dormant until rain stimulates hatching. The emerging nymphs form dense ravenous bands that inflict considerable damage to crops and pasture before maturing and flying to another area, laying eggs and repeating the damage elsewhere.

Mice plagues also occur after years of drought followed by good seasons. Mice can survive through long dry seasons, then rapidly increase in numbers when there is a good supply of food and moisture.

Plagues of mice and locusts have been recorded since biblical times, and both have been common in Australia. Until recently, explosions in mouse numbers were often followed by population crashes with minor activity during the following years, which prevented a build-up in numbers. However, recently mice have become a more persistent problem with populations continuing from one year to the next.

There was an outstanding season in the crop growing areas during 2020, and with excellent rainfall, the crop yields were near record highs. With so much grain, not all of it could be stored in sealed grain facilities, and much of it was held in open sheds. This provided a feeding bonanza for the mice and stimulated an explosion in numbers which reached plague proportions.

The usual approach for controlling the problem is the use of broadscale baiting with zinc phosphide. This goes some way to protecting crops but will never entirely prevent the plague, and a problem with zinc phosphide is it will also kill other animals if they consume the poison.

The recent mouse plague had been so severe that the NSW Government lodged an application to the Australian Pesticides and Veterinary Medicines Authority to use bromadiolone for broadscale mouse control. Bromadiolone is a potent anticoagulant rodenticide and is classified as an extremely hazardous substance in many countries. It is not approved for broadscale baiting in any other developed country, and it will kill almost anything that eats the poisoned mice or the poison itself.

Research has found lethal levels of bromadiolone in 31 species of birds, snakes, lizards, and native mammals and the broadscale use of bromadiolone is not recommended or supported by science. How irresponsible can a government be?

The planned control measures get worse. The same government that recommends using bromadiolone also supports a three-year genetic modification research program, led by the University of Adelaide, the CSIRO and The Centre for Invasive Species Solutions.

The program will test two strategies for population control using genetic modification of mice.

The first includes the 'X-shredder' approach, which eliminates sperm carrying the X chromosome. This produces more male than female offspring and, over time, is hoped to reduce the mouse population

The second is the 'female infertility' approach, which genetically modifies the mouse population so that all females that are produced will be infertile.

What could possibly go wrong?!

The unknown consequences of genetically modifying an animal and turning it loose on the planet are not only irresponsible but potentially dangerous.

Why do we manage our problems by trying to play God? This approach is no better than the failed pest and disease eradication programs that have been attempted since the green revolution. If something is a problem, we must kill it or modify it; we rarely look at what has caused the problem.

The grain-growing farmers of Australia have adopted industrial agriculture and produce wheat very efficiently, but the implementation of this form of agriculture requires wholesale clearing of grassland and woodland areas and the use of pesticides. This produces crops efficiently and cheaply but at great expense to the farm and regional ecosystems.

The grasslands and woodlands are a refuge and food

supply for predators of mice and locusts, and the loss of these areas also means the absence of birds, animals and reptiles that control the build-up of large numbers of mice. The use of pesticides to manage crop-damaging pests also kill wasps, fly species, mites, nematodes and fungi, all of which control locusts.

I am not suggesting that birds, animals, reptiles, insects, and mites can stop a full-scale plague but they can buffer against the very worst of these events by controlling local outbreaks. This effect has been observed in some areas during the recent mouse invasion. There were more mice than usual on Winona and neighbouring properties, but they were not a plague. This is because the district has mixed farming with grazing animals as well as wheat and oat crops, and much of the remnant areas of trees and grassland are intact. The mice have been controlled by predators in the grasslands and not allowed to breed to plague proportions.

When pesticides and poisons are added to an already dysfunctional landscape with very few predators, the pesticides will kill the last remaining predators, allowing mice numbers to increase to even greater numbers. Consequently, even more desperate steps are required to control the problem, and more potent poisons and genetic modification is seen as the only means of control.

We have not learned anything and continue to make the same mistake over and over again.

There are far-reaching challenges that confront our planet, which has declining ecosystems, degraded soil and changing climate, to name a few. It seems that they are insurmountable, but there is a groundswell of change happening around the planet. A growing number of people are becoming aware of the problems we are facing, and serious questions are being asked how we are going to fix this looming crisis. These questions are not coming from governments; in fact, most governments are still pretending nothing is wrong, and it is business as usual. The concerned people are from all countries of the world and all walks of life, from scientists, the man and woman on the street, and farmers.

Agriculture needs to be involved in the transformation that is required to fix many of the problems. It is the responsibility of producers to fix their agriculture practices that have been flawed for a very long time, so food and fibre can be produced without destroying farm ecosystems. Not only are the world farmers responsible for supplying food and clothing, but they are also capable of solving many of the environmental challenges that are facing the planet. By managing our farms well, we can also maintain plant and animal species diversity that create the ecological balance on which we are very reliant. Many of the world's environmental problems can be fixed by farmers and land managers because they own and manage a vast part of the earth's landmass.

I believe that Western society got agriculture wrong by following a flawed agriculture system developed over 10,000 years ago in Mesopotamia. The Sumerians from Mesopotamia created saline soil, dysfunctional soil, and deserts with their farming methods. We have continued to use the same basic methods of growing crops and running livestock that was initially developed in Mesopotamia, and never looked at how Mother Nature works, and the interconnectedness of everything in nature.

Modern industrialised agriculture appears to be an improvement on ancient farming practices, but mostly we have just replaced the 'oxen' with a tractor, and the 'Ard' with a bigger plough, then exchanged the plough for chemical herbicides. The increasing amount of fertiliser and pesticide that is regarded as essential in industrial agriculture is only necessary because the current production method of farming is broken.

· · ·

WOMEN IN AGRICULTURE

Until the green revolution, agriculture was about growing things, but modern agriculture has become very efficient at killing things. A vast array of poisons has been developed during the last seventy years to kill weeds, kill insects, and kill anything else that stops the relentless push of industrial agriculture. Agriculture and is no longer about nurturing the land and its animals.

It seems imprinted in the human male's mind of the need to kill things, and this mindset has spilled over into industrialised agriculture. Men have been the developers of new farming methods and agriculture is now about killing things with bulldozers, ploughs, and pesticides.

In other words *'We kill things that want to live and grow things that want to die.'*

Agriculture and the planet require people that are nurturers, not killers. By their very nature, women are nurturers who are excellent at looking after animals and are acutely aware of the dangers of poisonous substances and the need to protect human health. Consequently, women see the need for change and are more aware of the connection between healthy soil, healthy plants, and healthy humans. We need more women in agriculture because they will nurture the land and its soil. Agriculture needs more people like my great-grandmother 'Granny', who, over 100 years ago, managed the farm and nurtured the sheep with great care, starting a farming tradition that continues today in her descendants. Granny was instrumental in influencing her young grandson Harry, to also manage his sheep and farm in a nurturing and kind manner.

We need women involved in all forms of agriculture, from running farms, agronomists, and scientists, because women understand the need for change. It is extremely pleasing to see women purchasing farms in Australia, and many other countries, and being immensely successful at growing crops and raising animals, but most are doing it differently. They are adopting regenerative practices, using less or no pesticides, and restoring the grasslands and farm ecosystems.

What type of world do we want for our descendants? As Granny did in her era, and what we do today, will have a significant influence on our farms and planet, and whether they are suitable for our descendants.

During the last 30 years, making a living from agriculture has been tough, for many reasons. Variable climate, with droughts and floods, have always been challenging in Australia and most countries. My great grandparents Nicholas and Granny battled through the horrific 'federation' drought of the early nineteen hundreds with only a handful of sheep surviving. The drought finally broke with good rain, and with persistence and hard work, grew good wheat crops and slowly increased their sheep numbers. They were able to survive this terrible time, mainly because the soil and grassland were still intact, which allowed the farm and landscape to recover quickly.

Many farmers the world over are struggling more than ever because the soil on their farms has become degraded and lost its fertility, water holding capacity, and resilience. The grasslands that created rich, healthy soil and nurtured animals, crops, and farming families, are long gone. The perennial grasslands have been replaced with annual weeds and annual crops. The crops that are planted into the dysfunctional soil are propped up with large amounts of chemical fertiliser and plagued by disease, insects and weeds as never before. How did this happen, and why is it worse?

Over the last century, each generation has unknowingly taken too much from the land. Each generation has unintentionally degraded the soil and destroyed the grassland. The individual farmer and owners of the properties are usually not to blame; the farming and grazing methods used, are the primary cause of the decline in farms and farming families.

Like many good farmers in his era, Harry adopted innovative farming practices that repaired Winona and allowed him to be profitable, only to have the methods eventually decline in ways that he could never have foreseen. No one was aware of ecological farming problems in the 1950s. Now, in the 21st century, farming is as challenging as ever, but we have looming problems that have not been encountered before. The planet is undergoing modification in climate and with seasons and rainfall becoming more variable, farming around the world is going to become more difficult and far more financially risky. The industrial farming methods that have been adopted are already economically perilous because they have been created by companies that wish to make money from industrialised agriculture. To continue farming with an already risky model is committing financial suicide. For agriculture to be financially safer farmers, need to look at getting off the high-cost industrialised farming treadmill.

Agriculture has fed generations of humans for many thousands of years, but the type of agriculture western civilisations have developed has been plagued with problems from the beginning by destroying grasslands, creating deserts, saline soil, and acidic soil, the world over. Modern agriculture can produce a lot of food, but it has never taken into account the ecological and environmental cost to farms, ecosystems, and the planet. There is no point in producing a lot of food if the food is depleted in nutrients and the methods of producing food destroy the world on which we stand.

Many native people developed methods of producing food and clothing that sustained them for millennia. They did this by having great respect for nature and working within the confines of natural systems. These same native people learned to nurture the land and had immense respect for it. If we, as a species, are going to survive on this planet we will need to treat mother earth with the same type of respect.

How do we feed nine billion people in fifty years time? Scientific developments claim to have the potential to produce food for billions of more people, but the answer cannot be with more of the same. Not more of the failed green revolution, not more genetically engineered plants and animals, not more massive machinery. All of these may produce more food but because they do not take into account ecology and the environment they are destined to fail.

We should learn to live within the constraints that Nature puts on us and the planet.

To achieve this and be able to feed nine billion people, our farms need to function as ecosystems. If they function as ecosystems, they will produce plentiful food and fibre and protect our planet from potentially severe environmental problems.

These comments will alarm many farmers who say that it is imposable to fix environmental problems and be profitable but there growing numbers of farmers around the world that are very profitable and are also farming in an environmentally responsible manner. These people are using different methods to regenerate their properties and reduce pesticide and fertiliser inputs. Most are not organic farmers but are working within natural systems.

Many industrial producers know that their farming methods are not working well. They know that the increasing cost of growing crops and raising animals is making life difficult. They also know that the vast amount of money spent before a crop is planted make their farming methods financially risky, but it is not always easy to change.

Often farmers find themselves on a treadmill they cannot easily step off and are locked into using more chemical inputs and pesticides. If they stop using or reduce fertiliser and pesticide, crop yields will usually decrease, so to maintain production and profit, they are forced into continuing the use of fertiliser and pesticides.

Changing to a different form of agriculture can be financially risky because production can decrease as chemical inputs are reduced until an ecological balance is created, nutrients become available, and pests are managed biologically.

When I stopped using fertiliser after the 1979 fire, pasture production dropped, and stock feed declined because the Pasture on Winona was dependent on phosphorus fertiliser. It took a few years for the soil ecosystem to improve, nutrients to become available and Pasture to be productive again.

It may appear I am suggesting that all farmers and land managers are bad farmers and are doing severe environmental harm. Many farmers are doing an excellent job of managing their productive farms. These managers often operate different enterprises of sheep, cattle and crops on one property, but usually, do not integrate the enterprises. There are also cropping farmers that zero- till different crops which they alternate and rotate. They are heading in the right direction, but many do not fully understand, and are never told the vital importance of soil health and associated soil carbon. Many are also not aware of the necessity for more plant species diversity, to improve soil health and the farm ecosystem, which will reduce costs and increase profit.

It is not always easy for someone to change. To change is admitting to themselves and peers that they have been wrong for most of their life. Many people alter agricultural practices after a crisis like a drought or a flood. The reason I changed was that of fire. I had no choice but to change, and that change was in part responsible for the development of 'pasture cropping'.

The way many people get off the chemical treadmill of more pesticides and more cost is to transition off fertilisers and pesticides over time. When this method is used, crop and pasture yields can be maintained while the farm and soil ecosystems are restored. Even though it can be challenging to step away from mainstream industrial agriculture, there is now a trend away from it and toward regenerative agriculture by increasing numbers of farmers and scientists.

How can our farms function as ecosystems and produce food and fibre in the quantities required for the increasing number of people on our planet? It will surprise many that there are a lot of agricultural techniques being adopted around the world that are producing large amounts of food while regenerating farms and ecosystems. Farmers, not scientists, are developing most of these practices.

CLIMATE CHANGE

It is generally accepted that the earth's climate is changing. Many factors could induce change with the planet's climate, but the alteration in conditions is mainly due to increases in human activities such as the burning of fossil fuels (coal, oil, and natural gas) and agriculture. During the last one hundred years, changes include an increase in global average air temperature of 0.85 degrees Celsius, widespread melting of snow and ice, and rising global sea levels. The additional heat in the climate system has also affected atmospheric and ocean circulation, which influences rainfall and wind patterns.

The greenhouse effect is a natural process that warms the atmosphere and the Earth's surface in much the same way that a greenhouse traps heat, and enables plants to be grown in cold climates,

Greenhouse gases, which include water vapour, carbon dioxide, methane and nitrous oxide, trap heat from the sun by allowing it to penetrate the atmosphere. Some of the heat is reflected back to space, and the rest is absorbed and re-radiated by the greenhouse gases. This natural process is essential for life on Earth to exist by maintaining the planet's temperature. Without greenhouse gases, the average temperature of Earth's surface would be about 15 °C colder than the present average of 14 °C

The earth's climate is changing mainly because the earth's atmosphere has more greenhouse gas than usual, which trap heat in the atmosphere causing Earth's greenhouse effect to become more intense, but the majority of climate scientists now agree that human-induced expansion of the greenhouse effect is the primary cause of the current global warming increase.

Modern agriculture, food production, and distribution are significant contributors to greenhouse gases and associated changing climate, with agriculture being directly responsible for fourteen percent of total greenhouse gas emissions.

Tillage and excessive herbicide use create bare soil and deplete the carbon's soil, which reverts to carbon dioxide and returns to the atmosphere. With much of the world's cropping soil left exposed, and without plants growing for much of the time, there is no mechanism for soil carbon to be produced, consequently, much of the world's agriculture soils have declined in carbon by almost seventy percent. The loss of this much carbon from the planet's grassland soils would account for billions of tonnes of carbon which is now in the earth's atmosphere as carbon dioxide instead of in its soil as carbon. Every tonne of carbon lost from soil adds 3.67 tonnes of carbon dioxide to the atmosphere, which has increased atmospheric carbon dioxide by about forty percent since the Industrial Revolution.

Synthetic nitrogen fertiliser is a significant source of nitrous oxide emissions from agricultural soils. Nitrous oxide emissions increased by around twenty percent from 1990 and now make up twenty-three percent of greenhouse gases from agriculture. This has been driven by the excessive widespread use of nitrogen fertiliser to increase crop yields with intensive industrial agriculture practices.

· · ·

Restoring Water Cycles To Cool Climates

Reverse Global Warming

A growing number of scientists are looking at climate change from a different angle and are finding that increasing carbon dioxide is a symptom of something much larger. Australian scientist, Walter Jehne, has been quoted as saying that 'the elephant in the room has been overlooked because the elephant is too large to fit into the room'.

The elephant that won't fit in the room is water. Water is a planetary heat regulator that cools the biosphere of the planet, and if the worlds water cycles are restored, it can help address, destructive feedback loops in the climate system.

The 'Blue Planet's soil has the capacity to store vast amounts of carbon, but over the last one hundred years, poor agriculture practices have significantly reduced soil carbon, which has returned to the atmosphere as carbon dioxide. The often untold consequence of that is the loss of soil water. The deficiency of soil water is primarily due to a severe decline of soil carbon and its associated water holding and water storage capacity. This water ends up in the atmosphere as water vapour, and many millions of hectares around the planet have lost so much of the soil water, they have either become deserts or are rapidly desertifying with 40% of the planets agricultural soil now classified as 'degraded' in more than 160 countries.

Some of the reasons these areas have degraded are the destruction of grasslands due to poor grazing management. In more recent times, since the start of the 'green revolution in the early 1950s, the loss of soil carbon and increase in greenhouse gas has been caused by the manner crops have been grown with cultivation, heavy fertiliser application, and the use of pesticides.

The disturbance of soil with tillage destroys soil structure, kills soil microbes, and rapidly reduces soil carbon. The use of high fertiliser rates is detrimental to soil microbes, and when nitrogen fertiliser is used, nitrous oxide is emitted, which can have significant impacts on the planet's climate. Nitrous oxide is a potent greenhouse gas; that's around 300 times more effective at trapping heat than carbon dioxide, and it persists in the atmosphere for up to 114 years. The use of pesticides like insecticide and fungicide kills soil microbes, which are vital in building soil carbon. When all three are combined, they destroy the soil ecosystem, loses carbon to the atmosphere as carbon dioxide, the soil ecosystem becomes dysfunctional, and the soil simply becomes a medium for holding up plants.

Over the last 70 years, this growing crop method has reduced soil carbon levels from over six percent to less than one percent on many farms. To put this simply, the planets soil water and hydrological balance have been destroyed, and the water that used to be held in the soil is now in the atmosphere as water vapour. When water vapour is combined with the other greenhouse gases, it is inducing abnormal global climate changes via our changes to the Earth's natural heat balance through the greenhouse effect.

The consequences of industrial agriculture go even further. Soils left bare by over clearing vegetation or inappropriate cropping methods will absorb vastly more solar radiation than adjacent land with protective plant cover.

As the bare ground heats up, it often exceeds 70 degrees Celsius and re-radiates vastly more infrared heat back out into the air, which creates high-pressure heat domes that form over bare hot areas. These heat domes can block the inflow of cool, moist, low-pressure air, from the ocean into these hot regions which can impair rainfall and cause further aridification of these regions.

Before the European settlement of Australia in 1788, Australia's grasslands and ecosystems created soils that were soft and spongy. These carbon-rich soils were created over many millions of years by Australia's biota, which evolved highly efficient processes in which its soils could infiltrate, retain, efficiently use, and recycle every limited raindrop that fell. The prairies of the American mid-west had some of the best soils in the world that were also soft and spongy, but unfortunately, it took less than one hundred to reduce both countries grassland to dust-bowls, with the adoption of western industrialised agriculture.

Agriculture has been a large part of the planet's climate crisis and ecosystem decline, but it can also play a significant and vital role in fixing the problems, and that can be done by growing plants. These plants will need to be produced, not by using industrial farming, that caused many of the problems but by farming differently and using a great diversity of plants that always keep the soil covered with green growing plants. This can be done by growing diverse cover crops or with clever crop rotations, but the better way will be to restore ecosystems and grasslands into which we can sow a diverse range of crops using 'pasture cropping' techniques.

By growing plants, we know that soil carbon levels can be restored while removing carbon dioxide from the atmosphere, but an additional benefit of drawing down atmospheric carbon is that we can significantly cool the planet's surface to alleviate and even overturn the damage done by raised planetary temperatures.

I would like to thank Walter Jehne for help in contributing to this chapter of the book

Walter Jehne is an internationally recognised soil microbiologist and innovation strategist. He has immense field and research experience in soils, grasslands, agriculture and forests at local, national (CSIRO and Science Adviser to, Australia's National Soil Advocate), international (UN) level.

Walter has addressed many audiences around the world including 'Sequestering Carbon in Soil, Addressing the

Climate Threat Conference', Paris, May 2017, also presented at 'International Conference on Negative Co2 Emission's, Sweden May 2018 and Harvard University, April 2018.

It is often said that an expanding global population and our need for more food have inevitably led to an increase in synthetic nitrogen fertiliser use. The real reason for the increase in nitrogen fertiliser is declining soil health. As soil becomes degraded with inappropriate farming practices, soil carbon and associated soil nitrogen decline, necessitating the use of additional nitrogen fertiliser, which creates more nitrous oxide emissions further degrades the soil.

The removal of excess carbon dioxide from the atmosphere can be simple. Put it back in the soil where it belongs. This can be done by mimicking Mother Nature and growing an abundant and diverse range of plants. During photosynthesis, plants use carbon dioxide and water to make simple sugars. Through this process, carbon dioxide can be stored, or sequestered, in the soil as carbon, via root exudation and dead and decaying plants.

This natural process has enormous potential to restore balance in the planet's atmosphere and mitigate the effects of climate change. The benefits do not end with helping to fix the earth's climate. Increasing soil carbon can have other huge advantages, such as improving soil health, water-holding capacity, and nutrient cycling. All of these benefits reduce the production cost to the farmer and enhance the quality of food produced.

To achieve this, we need most of the world's farmers practising regenerative farming methods that restore their farm's soil ecosystems.

Winona's soil has been sequestering or storing carbon for many years. A recent property assessment was conducted which found the total amount of carbon dioxide that is being stored far exceeds the total emissions of carbon dioxide, methane and nitrous oxide by many thousands of tonnes.

This carbon is being sequestered, to some extent by trees that have been planted, but the majority of carbon dioxide is being removed from the atmosphere and transferred into the soil by Winona's grassland and stored as carbon.

The issue of changing climate on our planet has created considerable debate around the world. There is a growing revolt happening amongst the people of the world around inaction about climate change, and dispute about the consequences of not doing anything about it. I believe the debate about whether the world's climate is changing because it has been caused by us humans, or is a natural occurrence, is irrelevant. We need to stop treating our planet as a rubbish tip, by dumping our pollutants into the air, our garbage into the sea and rivers, and dumping excessive pesticides and contaminants and fertiliser, onto our agricultural land. This is the only planet we have – we should look after it.

INTERNATIONAL DEVELOPMENTS

I have always been searching for ways to further improve 'Pasture Cropping' and had thought that more species diversity would be beneficial for the crop and the soil.

The Winona grassland now had around 60 species which were improving soil structure, soil carbon, and nutrient cycling during the spring, summer and autumn months, but a majority of these species were dormant in the winter. A single species like oats, 'Pasture Cropped' into dormant grassland, stimulated soil during the winter months but was only one species. What would happen if I added more species with the oat crop?

In 2009 I started to plant a mix of oats and field pea as a winter crop. I immediately saw good results with improved grazing value and benefit from nitrogen the legume plants were adding, but I was searching for ways to increase soil carbon further and improve nutrient cycling. If I could achieve this, I may be able to reduce or eliminate the use of fertiliser that was applied to the crop.

In 2012 I had the privilege of being a Keynote Speaker at the 'No-Till On The Plains' Conference' which is a leading agricultural conference, in Salina, Kansas, USA. Part of that visit included a car trip to Bismarck, North Dakota to attend another convention. During that trip, I met some of the most influential farmers in the USA. Gabe Brown from North Dakota, David Brant from Iowa and Gail Fuller from Kansas are leading the way agriculture is practised in the USA with the development of 'cocktail cover cropping'. The methods they were using would be part of the answer to how I could improve nutrient cycling and soil health with 'Pasture Cropping'.

COVER CROPPING

'Cover cropping' had its origin as 'green manuring' which has been an agricultural practice among European farmers for more than two thousand years, and is believed to be an even more ancient practice in China. Green manuring is a system of growing a crop and ploughing it back into the soil while the plants are green. The main reason for this is to add organic matter and nutrients to the soil to benefit the following crop. This very successful custom has become less popular with the advent of chemical fertiliser, and its practice has almost ceased with the development of industrialised agriculture.

As good as 'green manuring' is, the crop is required to be ploughed into the soil, which eliminates much of the benefit done by the 'green manure crop'. Terminating the green manure crop without ploughing was developed to retain the benefits of green manuring without the adverse effects of ploughing. This terminated crop is called a 'cover crop' into which the main crop is zero- tilled.

Many different plants can be used as cover crops, but the

more common are legumes like peas, and cereal crops such as cereal rye. Cover cropping can be described as sowing an annual crop between periods of regular crop production with the primary purpose being to create thick mulch into which the following cash crop is planted using zero-till farming methods. The many benefits of a cover crop can be weed control, soil erosion control, increased soil fertility, improved soil health, and reduced crop pests and diseases.

Before the main crop is sown, the cover crop is terminated. Herbicide is often used to kill the cover crop, but a method growing in popularity is the use of a roller-crimper which reduces or eliminates the use of herbicide. A roller crimper has a large cylinder about 50 cm in diameter which has long fins running down the length of its surface. It attaches to a tractor and rolls over the field, pressing the crop onto the soil surface and killing the plants by crushing the stems. When terminated, the plants create a thick mat on the ground surface, which controls weeds, conserves moisture, and maintains soil temperature much like mulch in a garden. A cash crop is then sown through the mulch with a zero till planter running parallel to the roller's path, planting seeds directly into the soil without disturbing the thick mulch of the terminated cover crop.

Interest in cover cropping is gaining momentum. It is being used to combat some of the problems associated with conventional zero-till cropping techniques like herbicide-resistant weeds, declining soil carbon, declining water holding capacity, and poor nutrient cycling. The method is also being adopted by organic producers who see it as a way of growing crops without ploughing or using herbicide.

'Multi-species cover crops', sometimes referred to as 'cocktail cover crops', uses a combination of plants that consist of oats, cereal rye, or barley, legumes such as annual vetch and pea, and brassica like radish and turnip, are used instead of a single species cover crop. The crop mixture can consist of up to twenty plant species, which are planted together as a mix. The combination of vertical taproots and horizontal roots from the mix of species produces a 'three-dimensional' root network that a single species can never achieve. The more complex, diverse, and extensive the cover crop's root network is, the greater the improvement in soil structure, nutrient cycling, and organic carbon. This has a substantial positive effect on grain yield and health of the main crop that is planted in the surface mulch and diverse root mass of the cover crop.

Multi-species cover crops are much more stable and productive than monoculture crops because they are closer to mimicking naturally occurring diverse ecosystems like grasslands.

For decades ecologists have understood the importance of diversity in ecosystems, and know that plant species diversity create more biomass, are resistant to insect attack and disease, and create an environment where colonising annual weeds do not thrive

Contrary to the thinking of ecologists, advocates of industrialised monoculture crops require the removal of any plant, which is believed to deplete soil moisture and nutrients needed for a grain crop. This is not the experience of US farmers growing diverse, multi-species cover crops, and it is not my experience growing crops into diverse perennial grass that act as a perennial cover crop. The US farmers report better grain crops, vastly reduced soil water evaporation, less disease, less insect attack and improvement in soil nutrients after 'cocktail cover crops'

David Brandt from Carroll, in the state of Ohio, is most likely the leading crop farmer in the USA. He is often seen as the father of multi-species cover cropping in that country, winning many farming awards over the years. He was one of the very early adopters and pioneer of zero-till farming and has used this method to plant his corn, wheat, and soybean crops since 1971.

David has always been regarded as innovative. He had been practising zero-till since the early 1970s, and in 1978 he saw a reduction in his corn yields and tried cover cropping by adding hairy vetch and winter peas to the system to get more nitrogen. This worked well, and David began to look at how he could get further improvements. In the 1990s he started using mixes of cover crops into which corn or soybean was zero-tilled into the residue

Over the years David continued to experiment with multi-species crops and now uses over ten species ranging from tall plants as well as forbs and legumes in a multi-species mix.

This has shown exceptional improvement in soil structure, soil health and nutrient cycling. The cover crop mix has enabled David to significantly reduce fertiliser without any yield loss and saves over $100 an acre in fertiliser cost. Added to the substantial financial savings are excellent ecological benefits. The suppressive effect of the cover crops and improvement in soil health has reduced weeds in David's fields to a point where he has been able to cut herbicide use in half. Insecticides are no longer used because beneficial insects are drawn to his farm by insect attracting plants in the cover crop mix. Organic matter increase of over one percent per annum has been recorded, and crop yields improved with corn increasing by twenty-five percent, soybeans by thirty-five percent and wheat by a massive forty percent.

Like many farmers, David Brandt has learned about soil health and cover crops by trial and error on his farm. He is passionate about the benefits and educates many farmers around the USA by running field days on his farm and speaking at numerous conferences.

When I first met Gabe Brown, we were both amazed how similar our stories were and the reasons we changed from conventional industrialised farming. I had to change because a bushfire destroyed Winona and transformed my life. Gabe changed because of a series of hailstorms and drought transformed his life.

Gabe, his wife Shelly, and son Paul run the 5000 acre 'Brown Ranch', near Bismarck in the USA state of North Dakota. Gabe's story began in 1991 when he and his wife Shelly bought the ranch from Shelly's parents. The farm had been managed conventionally with monoculture crops of wheat, oats, and barley which were supported by the application of synthetic fertilisers and herbicides. Tillage and ploughing had been used to prepare the soil for many years, and the soil was like most that have been farmed in this manner, poorly structured with very little organic matter.

The first of Natures lessons that were to change Gabe's life happened in 1995 just before crop harvest when a freak hail storm destroyed the entire 1200 acre wheat crop. But it was after another hail storm the following year, a drought in year three, and another hail storm in year four that he started to think differently. As financially devastating as these natural disasters were, Gabe now believes that it was the best thing that could have happened because it changed the way he looked at industrial agriculture.

With only 15 inches of precipitation per year and much of that with snowfall, Gabe became aware of the importance of soil water holding capacity and soil health. He realised that a large part of his problem was the soil had become extremely degraded, and the ranch grew very little plant diversity. He also started to look at how nature functions with an extensive range of different plants and he began to model his farm on healthy native grassland that has lots of biodiversity.

To achieve this aim, Gabe sold all of his tillage equipment in 1993, bought a no-till drill, and now all the crops are planted using no-till farming. This was a major step forward, but he was aware that he needed more plant diversity to improve soil health and organic matter. To achieve that aim he started growing two and three-way crop blends such as sorghum, millet and cowpeas or hairy vetch, triticale and clover, but even that changed in 2006 when he met Brazilian cover crop researcher Dr Ademir Calegari.

Growing cover crops with multiple species blends, or 'cocktail mixes', had been used in Brazil since the 1970s to cover the soil and stop soil erosion and with this very long association with cover crops, Dr Calegari is probably the world's leading authority on cover crops. Dr Calegari spoke of the importance of growing multi-species blends consisting of at least six or seven species in a mix and Gabe immediately thought of diverse native grassland and realised that is the way nature functions. Since that time, Gabe started to increase the cover crop plants and now often uses 15-20 species, including broadleaf brassica, legumes, and cereal plants such as wheat and oats.

Cover crops, sown in this manner, are used for their soil health, soil structure and nutrient cycling benefits for the main corn crop, but Gabe saw the grazing potential of the crop mixes and started to graze them with cattle. At the time this was unusual in the United States because most cattle are fattened with grain in feedlots. Gabe had been grazing the pasture areas of the ranch using holistic grazing management, but when he started using grazing animals on the cocktail cover crops, the organic carbon of the soil on the Brown Ranch went to extraordinary levels of almost four percent which is close to native prairie soil of five percent organic carbon. Because of Gabe's management, the soil and Pasture on the ranch are thriving with life. The Pasture is now mimicking the diversity of that found in native prairies, and microbial tests show bacterial and fungal diversity had improved substantially.

The enhanced Pasture and soil biology has increased soil nutrients which have enabled Gabe to eliminate chemical fertiliser. The improved plant and soil ecosystems have encouraged beneficial insects and microorganisms, which mean there is no longer any requirement for insecticides and fungicides to grow crops. Genetically modified crops are not used, and corn planted into the cover crop residue produces crops that are 25% higher than the district average. The production cost is now less than half of conventionally grown corn due to savings in fertiliser and pesticide, and herbicide is rarely used.

The extra stock feed from the 'cocktail crops' and holistic grazing management has enabled Gabe to double cattle numbers now run on the ranch. Gabe and Paul have also increased the animal enterprises on the ranch and are currently raising grass-fed beef, sheep, chickens and eggs, turkeys and bees.

Much of the foodstuff produced on the farm is now sold directly to customers, and currently the Brown family sell grass-fed beef, grass-fed lamb, pastured pork, free-range eggs, honey and grass-fed goat meat to a rapidly growing group of customers.

About 1200 km south of Gabe Brown, near the town of Severy in Kansas, live Gail Fuller and his partner Lynnette Miller.

Gail is a 3rd generation Kansas farmer who grew up on the family farm near the town of Emporia. Lynnette is also from a farming background, spending her youth on her own family farm a couple of miles south of Olpe, in the Flint Hills of Kansas

Gail began farming at a young age and started growing 'Roundup Ready' soybeans in 1997 and 'Roundup Ready' corn the year it was introduced. In a quest to eradicate soil erosion, no-till practices were adopted, and he produced his first cover crop in 1997. Gail began his regenerative journey in 2002 after learning about the importance of soil and soil biology and the significance of plant diversity. Within five years he was planting twenty different crops in a five-year rotation and took no-till farming to the next level by growing cover and companion crops. These crops protect the soil from erosion, cycle nutrients, feed soil microbes and improve water infiltration.

This mix of cover and companion crops and holistically grazed cattle and sheep both add and cycle nutrients, showing that it is possible to 'grow fertiliser' and produce high-value grain with little or no inputs. Gail decreased nitrogen fertiliser inputs on his farm by ninety percent, and eliminated the need for phosphorus and lime. These methods were so successful the farms' organic matter increased from 2% to 7% over fifteen years.

Life's journey takes many turns and eventually, it was time for Gail and Lynnette to move on. In 2019 they downsized and relocated 90 kilometres south to a new farm nestled on the edge of the Kansas Flint Hills.

Gail describes the farm as a 162-acre oasis, having native prairie, timbered areas, a large market garden, and two small orchards. Even though they call the farm an oasis, they realise that the farm's soil is degraded and eroded with low organic matter created by years of tillage during the last owner's management. Gail and Lynnette know they can fix the property and soil very quickly because of their previous farming experience and plan to restore the farm in five years, where it took twenty years to restore the old farm.

To achieve this, they will demonstrate many types of regenerative agricultural production. These include livestock, vegetables, fruit, timber, and grains, and the use of Pasture Cropping on some of the property to produce grain for pigs and chickens and help speed the farm recovery from the years of ploughing and erosion.

Gail and Lynnette are adding as much diversity as possible to the farmland, orchard and garden, by planting cover crops in the orchard and perennial species to the farmland. These include raspberries, hazelnuts, currants, elderberry, cherry, spicebush, perennial herbs and wildflowers, which will be added to the farm's sale products.

To show that there is a lot more to Kansas than growing corn and soybeans, they have re-established their herd of dual-purpose British White cattle and Katahdin hair sheep. The sheep are very well cared for by Lynnette, who proudly referrers to herself as a shepherdess. As well as the sheep and cattle, they also run pigs, meat and layer chickens, and ducks.

They also grow a wide array of crops, and when crops aren't being produced, the soil is planted with multi-species cover crops, some of which have over 100 species of plants. All this diversity is vital to growing soil and restoring the soil ecosystem.

This chemical-free, organic farm sells its goods through the label 'Circle 7' by Fuller Farms and markets grass-finished beef and lamb, pastured pork, chicken, free-range eggs and honey. These products are sold through their farm shop, farm restaurant, markets and delivered to pick-up locations.

To demonstrate how quickly a farm can be regenerated, they are encouraging the farm to be used for research and education to show the link between healthy soil and healthy people. To achieve this, they have an on-farm education centre which is used to host events, as well as the renowned 'Fuller Field school', which I had the pleasure to present at in 2017

Below is a quote from Gail

Over the last 50 plus years, much of the food we eat, including organic, has lost much of its nutrient density. We believe that the huge loss is directly related to the management of soil. Mineral moves through the soil and into the plant through the soil microbiome. This microbiome is broken up by tillage and chemical use. This is why our emphasis is on soil. We have learned that following the template of nature has allowed us to repair the broken soil ecosystem. This allows us to grow nutrient-dense food without

hindering the next generations ability to do so. In the process, we have eliminated our dependence on herbicides, fertiliser, insecticides and fungicides. This allows our ecosystem to stay intact, ensuring Mother Nature will be working with us instead of against us.
    Gail Fuller

MULTI-SPECIES PASTURE CROPPING

After meeting the innovative USA farmers, I knew that 'Pasture Cropping' could be taken to another level. I thought that a mix of species sown as a crop would create higher quality stock feed when grazed, and the different plants with assorted root structures would help soil structure and nutrient cycling.

Cocktail cropping in the USA uses a mix of annual species which is planted as a cover crop and used mainly to prepare the soil and control weeds for the main crop, which is often corn. Until now, many of the cover crops were not grazed with animals except for a small number of people like Gabe Brown and Gail Fuller who are aware of the benefits of animals to the soil and for profit.

'Pasture Cropping' is perennial cover cropping. The cover crop is perennial grass which does not require re-sowing, as distinct from an annual cover crop that needs re-sowing each year.

'Multi-species Pasture Cropping' is different from cocktail cropping. The mix of plants is my crop, and the perennial grass, the cover.

In the first week of March 2013, I sowed my first Multi-species Pasture Crop with my son Nick's help. After grazing the area short with sheep, a mix of oats, forage brassica, annual vetch, and field pea was zero tilled into the grassland which had around fifty species of perennial grass and forbs. No herbicide was used, but a small amount of fertiliser was applied with the crop. The result was spectacular. The crop grew almost as high as the fence and produced an enormous amount of excellent quality sheep forage throughout the winter months. We planted more of Winona to Multi-species crops during the next year, but this time, turnips, a fast growing clover, and daikon radish were added to the other species bringing the total species planted to seven.

Daikon radish is a root vegetable that has been grown in Asia for centuries. It is starting to be used in cropping programmes for breaking up compacted soil and cycling nutrients by bringing them from deep in the soil via its large elongated taproot which can grow up to 2 feet into the soil. I was using the radish to fix some of the soil compaction problems created by the use of disc ploughs since the 1930s, but I also found that it is good stock feed with sheep preferring radish leaf to many of the other species.

The benefits of Multi-species Pasture Cropping did not end with good forage. The flowering plants of pea and vetch attract insects which control plant-damaging insects, and the addition of legumes increased soil nitrogen. The long tap-roots on some of the plants cycle nutrients from deep in the soil making them available to the existing crop, and accessible to a crop planted the following season.

I initially thought the multi-species crop would only be used for stock forage, and harvesting grain would not be possible, but I found that plants like brassica and pea do not tolerate being grazed as many times as oats. Consequently, after three grazing events spaced about one month apart, the sheep removed the brassica and pea, leaving oats to produce grain, which can be harvested.

In 2015 a Multi-species Pasture Crop was grazed lightly and all seven species allowed to produce seed. This crop was harvested as a mixture and seed re-sown as a mix in future years.

Since sowing Multi-species crops, I observed how well my

merino lambs grew and fattened on the crop, but I had no data on animal performance when grazing multi-species crops.

I could also see improved soil structure and suspected that the crop could be stimulating an increase in soil carbon.

To see if my observations were correct, I conducted a trial on 'Winona' in 2020, comparing a multi-species crop with a single species crop.

A paddock was halved with the erection of a fence and a multi-species crop sown on one half and a single species of barley on the other half. Both areas were Pasture Cropped and had equal treatment of fertiliser.

A mob of 450 merino lambs were halved and placed on each crop, grazed for three months and weighed monthly. The results were remarkable.

The lambs on the multi-species crop doubled the single species lambs' weight, which also doubled the financial profit.

Soil chemistry and carbon test were done before and after the trial started. The difference between the two was astounding, given the short time of eight months between tests.

The soil beneath the multi-species crop had shown a 21% increase in soil carbon, 125% increase in phosphorus (Colwell), a 16% increase in total nitrogen and 13% increase in calcium, while most minerals in the soil of the barley crop either reduced or did not increase.

An unseen benefit of Multi-species Pasture Cropping is that vegetables like turnip, radish and pea grow very well in a mixture that is zero -tilled into dormant grassland. This now creates the opportunity to produce large areas of vegetables at a very low cost.

There is excellent potential for greater production and profit with Multi-species Pasture Cropping. The grassland is grazed pre-sowing the crop, producing products such as meat and wool. Then a multi-species crop is sown into dormant grassland, which provides high-quality animal forage. Vegetables can also be harvested, and later in the season, grain is harvested from the crop. After the grain harvest, I also harvest native grass seed from the grassland, and then it is grazed with sheep. When all of this is combined, the production can be considerable. This type of vertical stacking of enterprises has the potential to produce massive amounts of food, including vegetables, and challenges the argument that genetically modified crops and increasing rates of fertiliser and pesticide are required to feed the world's growing population.

It is certainly possible to feed billions of people while restoring grasslands, soil, the world's ecosystems, and the planet.

In November 2013 I had a visit to Winona from Joel Salatin. Joel is known worldwide, often referred to as the world's best farmer, and the author of many books. Joel was accompanied by the well-known TV personality and the host of *Gardening Australia*, Costa Georgiadis, who has an infectious passion for plants and people. On that day, I found out that Costa also knew a lot about regenerative farming practices and gardening. The day was entertaining, with Costa being his usual jovial self and everyone learning a lot from each other, between fits of laughter.

Joel and his family own 'Polyface Farm' in the Shenandoah Valley, Virginia, where they raise livestock using holistic management methods and maximise production with an integrated system. The farm produces high-quality "beyond organic" meats, which are raised using environmentally responsible, ecologically beneficial, sustainable agriculture. Produce from the farm is sold by direct-marketing to consumers and restaurants. Joel describes himself as a "Christian-libertarian-environmentalist-capitalist-lunatic-Farmer" who puts high importance on healthy grass, where animals can thrive in a symbiotic cycle of feeding. Cattle are moved from one Pasture to another, and then chickens in portable coops are moved behind them and eat protein-rich fly larvae in the cow dung while fertilising the field with their droppings.

Joel has shown that a massive amount of food can be produced from farms without using industrialised agriculture, chemicals or genetically modified plants. The enterprises on Polyface Farm consist of grass-fed beef, pastured poultry, eggs, pork, and rabbits, all directly marketed to customers, with much of it being sold through an on-farm store.

During Joel's visit to Winona, he became interested in 'Pasture Cropping' and on return to his farm in the USA, implemented pasture cropping to fill a summer forage gap. The area was first grazed with cattle, then sowed a sudax and pearl millet mix with a zero-till planter, without herbicide or fertiliser. The pasture crop was a great success, with the area feeding 80 cows during the summer months.

These are examples of what is happening in regenerative or ecological agriculture in the USA but across the Atlantic Ocean in Europe, interest is emerging in different forms of regenerative agriculture, and cover cropping is being adopted.

In Australia, two hundred kilometres west of Winona, Bruce Maynard is developing a different form of agriculture on his property, 'Willydah', near the town of Narromine. In 1996 he developed a method of growing crops similar to 'pasture cropping' that he called 'No kill cropping'. No Kill Cropping is a method that sows crops into existing plant and litter cover without eliminating any other plants. It works on the complementary effects of diverse pastures rather than competition factors. It is a very low cost, flexible approach to crop-growing that gives growers flexibility throughout the growing season. Bruce and his wife Ros have planted much of their farm to an Australian native shrub call saltbush. The saltbush is planted in widely spaced lines in circular patterns, which act as more efficient windbreaks and also allow oats to be sowed between the rows. Saltbush is good stock feed, and when combined with the forage value of oats, provides excellent feed for the cattle and sheep that the Maynard family run on the property.

Bruce Maynard's farming operations demonstrate triple bottom line principles, where a balance between profit, soil and landscape function, biodiversity and healthy social life is achieved.

Three thousand five hundred kilometres to the west, in Western Australia, Ian and Dianne Haggerty own approximately 13,000 hectares (31,000 acres) of land in the central wheat belt, around one hundred and ninety kilometres north east of Perth. They did not always own 31,000 acres of land they started with a property of 1500 acres in 1994 and due to their excellent management and developing their unique method of farming called 'Natural Intelligence Farming', have built the property to over 30,000 acres

The Western Australian wheat belt could be described as some of the most challenging areas to farm on the planet, with recent annual rainfall averaging only 250 mm and much of the area consisting of light sandy soil. Consequently growing crops in this environment is difficult, and over many years have been produced using high rates of chemical fertiliser. Ian and Diane saw problems using chemical fertiliser and, against scientific advice, chose to grow their crops using biological products and worm leachate with zero- till crop establishment methods.

Ian and Dianne integrate a merino sheep enterprise with the cropping programme. These sheep have been bred specially for the Haggerty's environment. They are well suited to the areas with low rainfall and different plant species, performing well and producing merino lamb sold through selected outlets. As well as producing wool and lambs the sheep are incorporated into the cropping programme to begin the process of biologically inoculating the soil, control weeds and fertilise the soil with manure and urine.

The results of changing from chemical fertiliser to biological products have been dramatic. Wheat yields have increased and coinciding with this improvement has been a dramatic improvement in soil structure, water-holding capacity, soil nitrogen and soil carbon levels when compared to conventional cropping methods.

Diane and Ian Haggerty's comments sum up how they farm:

> *None of this would be completely effective without our understanding of the land as a living organism and our connection to its life cycle. As we contribute to it, we live from it; we live with it - we must understand its nature and its inner life, what it gives to us and what it needs from us to work on our behalf."*

There is good adoption of better grazing management methods around Australia, and improved crop rotations are being implemented, but there has been minimal interest in annual cover cropping. In a country that is severely limited by degraded soil, and variable rainfall, it is something that needs addressing.

Criticism has come from scientist and agronomist in Western Australia saying that annual cover cropping will not work in that part of Australia because these crops will not grow through the very dry summers. That could be correct, but they fail to realise that 'Pasture Cropping' is actually 'perennial cover cropping', and the technique is working well in that part of Australia. In Western Australia, 'Pasture Cropping' is being implemented by first planting warm-season grass species, into which crops are being zero -tilled during the winter. An example of 'Pasture Cropping in

Western Australia is on Grant Bain's property. Grant farms 1400 hectares south-east of Geraldton where he grazes cattle on subtropical perennial pastures. Grant has been 'Pasture Cropping' into these pastures with barley and lupins to increase winter cattle forage without destroying the perennial Pasture. The results have been very successful and have shown that 'Pasture Cropping' can produce good stock feed, increase the productivity of perennial grass stands, and provide profitable risk-free options by getting grain harvest and excellent forage benefits.

Keith Tunney farms a 1300 ha property on near Dongara on the Western Australian coast, about three hours north of Perth, on which he runs about 2000 sheep and 500 head of cattle. Keith describes his soil as 'gutless sand' which is a result of the formation of ancient sand dunes created aeons ago. The sandy soil is nutrient-depleted, and growing crops in the area has been regarded as unviable for many years.

To produce more reliable stock feed, he replaced annual pasture species with subtropical, warm season, green panic and Rhodes grass, into which he planted tagasaste (lucerne tree) in alleys with 15-metre row spacing. During winter, he Pasture Crops' lupins or barley into the perennial grass between the rows of tagasaste. The results have been impressive with livestock being offered a three-course meal of tagasaste, perennial grass and Pasture cropped lupins and barley.

In most years, lupins and barley are harvested for grain, with grain yields shown to yield better than the district average and the added bonus of having green perennial grass to graze after crop harvest. By expanding and integrating his production system, Keith has been able to turn his 'gutless sand' into a very profitable farm. The integrated system regenerates his farm, adds and cycling nutrients to the sandy soil, and adds essential protection to the fragile landscape.

From 2008 to 2013 the 'Future Farm Industries Cooperative

Research Centre' EverCrop project has evaluated the viability of Pasture Cropping into different subtropical species at a focus site south-west of Moora Western Australia.

During five years of the project, it evaluated grain yield and biomass production of Pasture Crop barley and lupin, zero till sown into subtropical, warm-season grass, called Gatton panic. It was compared to barley zero tilled into areas that had no perennial grass species and planted with full herbicide application. The Pasture Crop area was treated with herbicide to control weeds but not kill the perennial grass.

The results were:

> Results to date have been very promising for both barley (2009, 2011) and lupin (2010, 2012) crops with little or no yield penalty (0-15%) in Pasture Crops when fertilised in line with district practice (Ward et al. 2012) During the trial the 'pasture crop' barley yield up to 4.3ton per hectare in 2012 and 'pasture crop' treatments yielded over 2t/ha of grain in 2013.
>
> Pasture Cropping systems can also lift overall biomass production, improve the feed value of stubbles, provide out of season fodder, and reduce the likelihood of wind erosion and groundwater recharge on deep sandy soils.

The conclusion of another trial (Caring for our Country project.) in Western Australia Pasture Cropping' report 2014

> Pasture Cropping' appears to offer flexibility to switch between crop and livestock production, and greater stability in income across years relative to annual-pasture/annual-crop rotations.
>
> Analysis based on 2012 results (decile 1 year) showed that three years of Pasture followed by one year of 'pasture cropping' out performed conventional crop/annual pasture rotations by around $60/ha or $15/ha/yr (Hagan et al. 2014).

There are a diverse group of excellent farmers presented in

this book. However, many more farmers and landowners are doing great things around the planet. They are all restoring their farms in different ways, although the manner in which they are doing it all has a similar outcome. They are all developing and adopting practices that function close to natural design. This has not only allowed them to regenerate their farm, farm ecosystem and soil ecosystem; it has also enabled them to be more profitable.

Most of the farmers who are developing and adopting practices that regenerate farms are also passionate about the need to change. Many are also educating fellow farmers about better farming practices.

There is a groundswell of change happening around the planet. However, this growing group of excellent farmers represents an alarmingly small percentage of farmers. The increasingly high levels of fertiliser, pesticides, and genetically modified crops used in industrial agriculture make multinational companies wealthy while putting severe financial pressure on many farmers, destroying their farm ecosystem while producing food that is increasingly unsuitable for human consumption.

WINONA

My life story starts on the 16th December 1979 because almost everything preceding that dreadful, windy, and hot day was eliminated. The Winona that Harry and Mari created was gone, taken away by the fire that is an all too familiar occurrence in Australia. All of their life's work, except for Winona's soil and a handful of their precious sheep that survived, were reminders of a lifetime of dedicated work. The creation of the Merino Stud, decades of fencing, designing and building the Winona homestead, woolshed, and farm infrastructure, were all destroyed. It is ironic that the development of the pasture and fertiliser programmes, that worked so well during the 1950s and 1960s, eventually contributed to making the fire so fierce by creating dead, dry Pasture during the summer months. From that day, everything changed, it had to, everything was wiped out, and the previous methods could no longer be afforded. But out of the catastrophe came something that could never have been imagined. A method of practising agriculture that had never been thought of, that had the potential to change agriculture around the world.

Pasture Cropping has been adopted by over 3000 farmers worldwide, managing an estimated one million acres in Australia, the USA, South Africa, South America, and Europe to grow crops and restore grasslands, farm ecosystems, and soil.

On Winona, crops are no longer grown using soil destroying ploughs, which rip apart the soil, killing its very life. Crops are grown by mulching the paddock, adding nutrients and biologically priming the soil with sheep. A narrow slice is cut through the dormant grassland and seed placed into the small slot. The result is a grain crop and restored, invigorated grassland and soil. Winona is now managed with similar numbers of sheep but grazed in a different, more natural manner, in large mobs rotating around the property, adding a pulse of nutrients and mulching the leftover grass onto the soil surface as they go.

Today, the property has soil that more closely mimics the original grassland soil, which stores carbon because plants remove carbon dioxide from the air and transfer it deep into the soil as carbon. The rehydrated soil, which has grown to twelve inches deep in parts of Winona, is covered with a thick, life-protecting layer of mulch created by the grassland laying the last seasons, dry grass, onto the soil surface. Nutrients that are essential for plant and animal growth are no longer supplied by tonnes of fertiliser that devastate soil microbial diversity. The nutrients are provided by plants, extracting minerals from deep in the subsoil, and bringing them to the soil surface, and billions of microorganisms continue the natural creation of nutrients by releasing minerals from the parent material in the soil.

The appearance of Winona had changed from resembling a European farm in the 1950s with short, green clover and ryegrass to Australian grassland sixty years later. This grassland is approaching the quality of 1880s grassland with an ever-increasing number of plant species which one day will match the species diversity of Nicholas and Granny's original property.

I feel all I have done is to encourage Mother Nature to fix the problems by farming and grazing in a way that works with her. Mostly I have merely stepped out of the way and let Mother Nature do her work.

My thoughts are with my sixth-time grandparents William and Eleanor, who have been farming in Australia since the early 1800s, after seventeen-year-old William stole a shirt, was given free passage to Australia and granted a fifty-acre farm in the fledgling country. Later in the 1860s, Nicholas and Grannie carved their farm out of what must have seemed a wilderness, and I am in awe of what every generation has achieved before me as I watch my three young grandsons playing the same games as I did on the property that I grew up.

It is hoped that they will not be tempted by the bright lights of the cities but settle for a quieter, but very satisfying life, amongst the grasslands of Winona.

ACKNOWLEDGMENTS

Writing this book has been a mammoth but enjoyable task, and without the help of many people, it would have been more difficult.

Foremost among the many people to thank are my Father, Harry and mother, Mari, for theirgreat wisdom.

My friend Daryl Cluff for his great ideas, inquisitive mind, and amusing sayings.

Dr Christine Jones, who inspired me to continue my work in developing 'pasture cropping' past a concept, and her support and clarification of the science behind 'pasture cropping', grazing management, and soil health.

Alan Savory for his input to this book, but more importantly, his work with the development of Holistic Management and grazing methods that are an essential component of 'pasture cropping'.

Many people have contributed, including Mike and Regina Byron, Sue Ogilvy, Elizabeth Farrelly, Racheal Treasure, and Elaine Timson, for her support and encouragement.

My international friends, Gabe Brown, Gail Fuller, and

David Brandt, who shared ideas that have contributed to this book, and my friend, the late Brian Lindley, whose jovial, friendly manner and excellent organisation skills brought us all together.

www.ingramcontent.com/pod-product-compliance
Lightning Source LLC
Chambersburg PA
CBHW052110030426
42335CB00025B/2921